T0018553

House to Home

Designing Your Space
for the Way You Live

Devi Dutta-Choudhury, AIA

ROOST BOOKS

Roost Books
An imprint of Shambhala Publications, Inc.
4720 Walnut Street
Boulder, Colorado 80301
roostbooks.com

Cover and interior illustrations: Jacqueline Alcántara
Cover and interior design: Debbie Berne

9 8 7 6 5 4 3 2 1

First Edition
Printed in China

♾ This edition is printed on acid-free paper that meets the
American National Standards Institute Z39.48 Standard.
♻ Shambhala Publications makes every effort to print on
postconsumer recycled paper. For more information please visit
www.shambhala.com.
Roost Books is distributed worldwide by Penguin Random
House, Inc., and its subsidiaries.

Library of Congress Cataloging-in-Publication Data
Names: Dutta-Choudhury, Devi, author.
Title: House to home: designing your space for the way you live /
    Devi Dutta-Choudhury, AIA.
Description: First edition. | Boulder, Colorado: Roost Books, an
    imprint of Shambhala Publications, Inc., [2020]
Identifiers: LCCN 2020031114 | ISBN 9781611808360
    (hardcover; acid-free paper)
Subjects: LCSH: Dwellings—Remodeling. | Architects and
    builders. | Architecture, Domestic. | Interior decoration.
Classification: LCC TH4816 .D865 2020 | DDC 690/.24—dc23
LC record available at https://lccn.loc.gov/2020031114

Dedicated to:

Mike, who convinced me that we do need doors

(and then installed them)

H, who got the nicest bedroom, twice

P, who taught me how to make friends with contractors

K, who restored my faith in *hugh-manatee*

Contents

House to Home

Introduction

I like to think of myself as a modern person. Like most anyone living today (or at least reading this book), I was raised in contemporary society, some urban and some suburban and even a little global. And I am a product of modernity, which includes everything from indoor plumbing to democracy. When it comes to your home, what does *modern* really mean? Homes should make our lives easier and be conducive to the ways we live today. Our lives are typically complicated, with working parents, kids in school, social networks to maintain both virtually and in real time, and, ultimately, a desire to keep it all together. We are busy, and we are connected to a larger world. We spend time with our families and strive to keep them functional. We cook *and* eat out. Our tastes are both general and specific. Yet, our complex lives have some very simple spatial needs. Our physical homes are the link between these disparate and converging aspects of our lives. This is modernity, and our homes should be designed to support it.

While I will always promote modern principles of design such as large windows, clean lines, and seamless transitions, I don't want to create a stylistic dogma with this guide. There are many styles out there, and I don't want to pigeonhole myself or you the reader by advocating any particular style. Most of us are into a lot of different home styles, or we're just thankful for a home at all. We may remember the New England colonial, or high-rise apartment, or commune in Oregon that we grew up in—but we also incorporate style we've picked up along the way. The set of *Mad Men* was so lauded not just because it captured the midcentury modern era so completely, but because if you look closely, there are items from the many decades preceding the midcentury ones. A 1920s lamp may sit alongside an Eames chair. An old oil portrait hangs near modern Nelson lamps. That's how most people live. It's rare to buy your home and furniture all at once. You buy a house. You live with a mattress on the floor or steel frame while you save up money or find the bed you want. (Or in our case, wait for your husband to finish making a handmade bed frame.) Then you add a vintage cabinet your mother leaves you. Then you buy an IKEA dresser because it works and it looks good. This is how style emerges for most of us. Our homes are a representation of our lives thus far, so it may not always match. I'm here to tell you that's okay! Homes are organic and dynamic and should allow change. But when we improve our homes, we can create the space we need to live our modern lives, and that's not about style, it's about life.

This book is a rough guide to improving your home through the lens of my family's experience in creating our own sort-of-modern home in California, which is still a work in progress. My husband and I were a young working couple with a two-year-old daughter, looking to buy a home. This was in San Francisco in 2004, so the options in our budget at that time were to buy a TIC (tenancy in common) flat in an old Victorian (San Francisco's version of a co-op) or look farther afield to get more space* for less money. We ended up across the Bay in Berkeley, California. Berkeley was a place I had visited and was sort of intrigued by. It was at its core a college town, but it also had many other aspects. It had a reputation for good food, good schools, and free speech, not necessarily in that order—and yet I was very skeptical about leaving the

*Actually, we didn't get more interior space, but we got more land around our home than we would have had in the city.

city for the burbs, so to speak. When we found this sweet little house in the hills, I was certain we would just do a quick renovation, live here for a few bucolic years, then come back to a city home when we could afford it. This has not happened—we ended up so immersing ourselves in this home, our neighborhood, and the city around us that we are literally a part of Berkeley now. For better or for worse, I couldn't imagine it any other way.

Even though I was not desperate to live in Berkeley at first, once I saw the house and the neighborhood, I was drawn to it immediately. This book is peppered with the details of our home, but essentially, it was a major fixer-upper—and that is being generous. The real estate listing even said, "bring your contractor!" From the conversations we overheard from other potential buyers, the consensus seemed to be that this house should be torn down. It was in a good, though secluded, neighborhood, but it did not have that instant curb appeal that can draw you in. A gate with a broken hinge was the first thing you saw from the street. A rotted trellis heavy with a bramble-like planting covered the front door. But once you got in, you could see the potential, and the essential qualities of a good home were all there. My husband and I put an offer on the house during that fast rise to the boom of the housing market and were lucky enough not to be caught up in a bidding war. No one else really wanted this house and all of the work it would take to improve it. Our offer was accepted, and so began this journey.

We embarked on a major renovation and addition during the subsequent recession (while our family went through a boom of its own, adding two more kids to our brood), so our perspective adjusted accordingly from cautiously visionary to relentlessly practical. We took that little 712-square-foot fixer-upper, added the space we needed, and created a place for our family to grow and change comfortably. I would call our house style "open book." You walk into the living space (which is an open plan, interconnected living/dining/kitchen/laundry), and the mechanisms of our lives are pretty apparent. It's a working home that shows and supports how we live. As an architect, I definitely had some strong notions of what this place should be—but those notions evolved dramatically as the project was underway. I imagined some magazine-worthy space created with sustainable practices and innovative materials, yet after living in the home for a couple of years I realized what we actually needed. This book is a chronicle of how we got there.

If you're reading this book, you're probably already thinking about home improvement, casually noticing things you like—or lack—in your space. Or perhaps you're already in the thick of things, talking to architects, creating Pinterest boards, binge-watching home improvement shows. I'd like to help by giving you this authentic account of my process. Yes, I'm an architect, and even I had struggles! I've also helped many other families in my professional practice with their own homes, and I learn something new from each project. We are all different, and the journey of home improvement will reflect that. It will bring out your best and your worst, sometimes all in the same day, but hopefully the end result will be that you have a space that is authentic and embodies who you are and helps you live your life. I hope this book helps you get there.

·　　·　　·
·　　·　　·
·　　·　　·

chapter 1

So you're looking for a place to live.

Choosing the home you will live in is your first opportunity to think about home improvement. You may not find "the one" you want off the shelf, but you can make it the one that works.

Modern living.

What are you looking for in your new home? The list may include style, square footage, neighborhood walkability, and a view. You may also have noticed that certain house types tend to encourage certain lifestyles. The shotgun homes of New Orleans and railroad apartments of New York City with rooms laid out enfilade force a sort of communal coexistence, since everyone in these places is constantly bumping into everyone else. This typology is a domesticated version of the bustling urbanity outside. New England's colonial homes and their midwestern progeny were originally designed to have ceremonial entryways, flanked by often-deserted but beautiful formal rooms. This layout suggests a life of privilege and austerity that is not as prevalent in today's world. San Francisco's Victorians allow a great deal of privacy and autonomy—maybe too much. Housemates can retreat into their rooms down a dark hallway, scarcely being seen. In the sprawling West, mission- and craftsman-style homes abound and seem to have a place for everything, with their great built-in cabinets and carefully defined and connected spaces, but these often offer little room for growth since they are so tightly designed. Even the suburban-development home with its laundry list of amenities and features can predetermine lifestyle aspects, such as primarily entering your home through the garage so you don't often see your neighbors. Yet none of these home types are immutable. We still manage to live out our modern lives in these places. We can make these homes modern.

When I say "modern," what comes to your mind?* The word *modern* started being used to describe architecture in the twentieth century. The meaning has evolved and become muddled over the years—do you mean early modern Art Deco style? Midcentury modern, a style that emerged after World War II and that still seems to resonate with homeowners today? Or do you mean the eighties' modern of bachelor pads with black leather couches? Or today's modern of clean lines and neutral palettes with Scandinavian influences? It's a word that changes meaning with every new decade's sense of modernity. For the context of this book, I just mean a home you can live in today. Modernity is about accepting ourselves and the way we live our modern lives as normal. Being modern doesn't mean your house style takes precedence over how you actually live. It means it is functional and has modern amenities and supports your modern existence. Your home should allow you to live that life with ease and pleasure.

We can make our lives easier when we update our homes to accommodate how we really want to live today. We all can and do live modern lives in homes that may be defined by real estate agents as something else, so instead of quibbling about nomenclature I say let's get on with living! We are not medieval, we are not dynastic, and most of us are not even renaissance in our daily lives. *We are all modern.* So buy that

*Le Corbusier, an early modernist architect who was kind of the Madonna of modernism (single name and all), proposed a new order for homes based on five elements that are still popular today: a free floor plan (basically what we call an "open plan" today), a free façade (windows and doors based on function rather than symmetry or tradition), *pilotis* (columns that held the home up off the ground), horizontal windows (to relate to the landscape rather than the human body), and a roof garden (to replace the land sacrificed below).

craftsman bungalow or midcentury prairie and, with some effort, you will manage to make it what you need.

The fundamentals for modern living are fairly basic. What do each of these mean to you?

SHELTER

A mix of spaces for both privacy & community

ACCESS

Easy relationships between spaces & to the outdoors

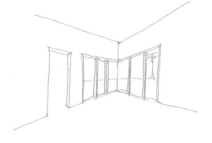

LIGHT

Abundant natural light & fresh air

Find a place with potential or find potential in the place you have.

We bought our house when we were still in our twenties (okay, I was twenty-nine and three-quarters, and my husband was about a month away from his thirtieth birthday when we moved into this home with our three-year-old) and we sub-consciously took to heart that old real estate adage, "buy the worst house in the best neighborhood you can afford." And did we ever. The house was a "charming" 712 square feet, with a 6-foot-wide galley kitchen without a refrigerator or range, two 9-by-9-foot bedrooms, a tiny sea-foam green bathroom, and a catchall room for everything else—eating, living, play-ing, and most often complaining about lack of space. To top it all off, the house sat precariously on eight skinny redwood posts on a large but steep down-sloping lot in the Berkeley Hills—just a stone's throw from the Hayward Fault. Stories of the impending Big One were seared across my mind. I braced myself against a door every time a passing truck rattled the house. I cringed every time our active toddler jumped too high or too hard. Could a twenty-five-pound child really bring down this fifty-year-old house? I thought so.

Granted, this was an incredible neighborhood nestled among rolling hills and oak trees, with sinewy, slope-hugging streets. It included both 1950s worker-type housing like ours and some of the oldest and largest historic homes in the city, not to mention the spectacular views of the Golden Gate—from our neighbors' houses. In fact, if you stand at the very far edge of our deck, peering over the edge while gripping the railing, you can catch a glimpse of the San Francisco Bay toward the North Richmond oil refineries. I'll take it!

The neighbors were mostly elderly, which we found somewhat reassuring. It meant that people moved here and liked it enough to stay forever. There was definitely a vibe of lingering hippieness; there were naturalists and academics with happy, wide grins aplenty. But it was almost unnervingly calm. Moving away from the bustling hipster Mission District in San Francisco was attempted social suicide; we were isolating ourselves in an aging neighborhood far from any real rapid public transportation, though a bus ambles along every half hour or so. Instead of the din of police sirens, live music, and that intoxicating urban mayhem of our old neighborhood, we had cackling blue jays and rustling leaves. We were dodging low tree branches instead of entrepreneurial *Street Sheet* salesmen. We could walk to a big old climbing rock instead of our favorite corner bar. But we saw something in this little house on stilts, and it wasn't a teardown as it was advertised. The ceilings were natural blond wood, the floors were oak, light came in from all four sides and, the kicker for us, the house faced true north, a fact we found particularly interesting since the property itself did not face true north. This house was a compass! Oh, and did I mention the deer? We thought the realtor must have scattered apples and salt licks around the yard for the open house because a little family of deer were just hanging around the yard every time we looked out of a window. We were sold on this house. Never mind that the only house in our San Francisco neighborhood we could afford to buy had belonged to a murder victim.* We would make this cracker box our home.

*True story: Our very sweet realtor was trying to find us a home in San Francisco within our "challenged" budget and showed us a lovely home with one fatal flaw: the last owner was murdered in it. Hard pass.

In retrospect, we were quite lucky to buy when and where we did. The market since then has tightened to the point that multiple offers from eager buyers on various homes can go unanswered and you're lucky to get any home in some metro areas. And these days, that home is probably not all you envisioned, but I see this as an opportunity instead of a liability.

If you already own a home that you want to improve, start from a positive perspective instead of dwelling—ahem—on what's lacking. Even if your home was not your first choice or even a choice at all, even if you moved into your parents' place, I believe every home has redeeming qualities. You may need to look really hard to find it, but there is definitely a kernel to build around. What *is* working about the place? Do you love the light? The bedrooms? The spacious garage? The way the rooms connect? Maybe even a really great—ummm—closet? Your home must at least provide shelter from the elements. It may take a year or more of living in the space before realizing what really needs to change. What can be done to make your house the home you cherish? In our case, in addition to the things I already mentioned, I really appreciated that there was no unfunctional space. Every spot had its job—no excessive hallways, no funky pop-outs, no niches—just clean lines with large plate glass windows so I could see the deer. In other words, it was *modern*.

To keep these exceptional traits of our little home, we planned an addition that would meet our spatial and structural needs without sacrificing the efficient beauty of the original house. The addition slid right under the old house, literally supporting it without destroying it. The house would look exactly the same from the street as it did when it was built in 1954—a stealth addition. And we could rest assured that our children could jump and dance and run without bringing down the house, at least not literally.

What you love about your home is the seed of what you can build on. Even if what you love is simply the neighborhood and the home itself is unremarkable, you build on that neighborhood by making the home an integral part of it. Maybe big sliding doors open onto a shared yard with a neighbor, or the front door opens onto a new stoop that invites someone to sit and chat for a minute. Windows that glow from the street in the evenings show that a home is inhabited and welcoming. There are architectural moments that make a neighborhood what it is. So, find that moment in the home that already speaks to you and let it grow.

There are three things that I think are the most important to look for in a new home:

#1 LOCATION, LOCATION, LOCATION

This includes the greater metro area as well as the local neighborhood and street, and the immediate neighbors. The neighbors that moved in next door to us actually called me before they decided to buy the house just to get a sense of the neighbors. I thought that was very smart. Other ways to assess the location qualities may be intuitive to some, but who doesn't love a checklist?

- ☐ Is it close to work?
- ☐ Is it close to amenities like grocery stores or farmers' markets, gyms, or other frequently needed spaces?
- ☐ Are there local parks for hikes, dogs, or kids?
- ☐ Does it look like the neighbors get along?

#2 SOLAR ORIENTATION

Does the home face the sunny south, or cool north? Ideally the home has at least two sides of windows, but if you are looking at a flat in a multiunit building you may just get one side of windows, making which side you face that much more important. If there's a choice, choose sun. Or, if you are a visual artist, you may choose north. These are light qualities to consider:

- ☐ Does the space you will spend the most time in face the sunny side of the home, or could it with some renovations?
- ☐ Does the outdoor space get good sun, considering gardening and gatherings?
- ☐ Are windows well sized?
- ☐ Are there walls without windows where you could add openings? Notice if you may be close to the property lines where windows are more restricted.

#3 SIZE

I don't mean number of bedrooms and bathrooms, but actual square footage and lot size. Some homes are divided up in a way that can be improved if the square footage is adequate. I don't want to put a specific size on this list, because everyone's comfort level with space is different. There are micro-units of 250 square feet that are perfectly fine for one urban dweller, while 250 square feet is the size of the closet for another.

- ☐ Does the square footage align with your needs for the home?
- ☐ Do rooms feel over- or undersized?
- ☐ Are there extraneous or unused spaces like dead-end hallways or duplicate rooms such as a den and a family room?
- ☐ Is there outdoor space to expand out or up to a second floor?
- ☐ Is there an unused garage or basement?

Notice I didn't include style on this list, because I think this is a mutable concept and it's more difficult these days to get exactly what you want. You are usually limited by what is actually on the market at the time you are looking for a home. Of course you will be drawn to certain charms of different homes, I just don't want homes ruled out if they can be updated to work for you. In my professional work, we've completely transformed homes with improvements that at least have those first three items covered.

Climate change—yes, I'm talking to you.

Even the most well-intentioned homeowner can start to lose sight of climate goals when it comes down to the bottom line. How can my cute little house contribute to climate change? I'm sad to say it does. Homes are the largest source of energy use in developed countries, so we need to be mindful of the impacts we have and will continue to have. Consider your home as part of a global effort from when you first start looking for a home. Location is the first front of climate action. If you live far from transit and amenities such as grocery stores, banks, schools, and jobs, you are at an immediate carbon disadvantage because, presumably, you will be driving to all of those locations in your car. Second, density is inherently more climate friendly. The sprawling acreage of rural areas is certainly appealing from some vantage points, but being near city centers has a climate edge. There are efficiencies of scale in delivering utilities and services to urban homes, and the less you have to get in your car to get somewhere, the better off we all are.

So, neighborhood and location are the first consideration from a climate perspective. Zoom into the scale of where you live, and there are similar rules of thumb. An apartment in a multiunit building is more climate-friendly than a stand-alone single-family home. A single-family home in a dense neighborhood is more climate-friendly than a sprawling neighborhood far from public transit. And so on. Bikeable and walkable neighborhoods are an obvious plus.

This doesn't mean you need to limit your search neighborhoods to expensive city centers, but you can look for the hyper-local amenities—is there at least a small strip on a nearby local street with a corner store, a decent restaurant, or market where you can get last-minute eggs or sugar? The daily trip count in and out of your neighborhood is an important factor from a climate perspective. A local park will at least provide a space to play and exercise without driving.

On a map, our house looks geographically close to amenities—when we were looking around the neighborhood for the first time, I could have sworn that little coffee shop near the UC–Berkeley campus was within easy walking distance from the new house. Coming from an urban neighborhood and having a serious coffee habit, I thought this was all I needed to be happy with the new house. But alas, the steep terrain meant that this "local" coffee shop was actually a twenty-minute walk—not exactly what I'm ready for *before* coffee. So, I learned to make coffee at home. There's a park just down the street, which has been an incredible boon to my three kids at all stages of life. Our house is ostensibly less than a mile to grocery stores and my kids' elementary school as the crow flies, but in reality, the vertical distance is a five-hundred-foot incline—not exactly walkable. But we can *take* walks—aimless, wandering walks where we may run into a neighbor or come upon a flock of wild turkeys. This was a lifestyle adjustment that has been for the best.

Acknowledging climate change requires identifying the best places to live:

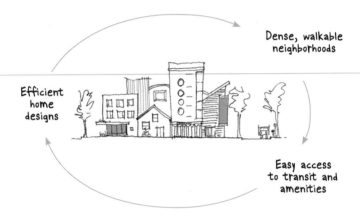

Dense, walkable neighborhoods

Efficient home designs

Easy access to transit and amenities

The next climate front is the home itself. Again, density is your friend. A compact layout is certainly more efficient than endless home sprawl. Grouping similar spaces so they can be heated and cooled at the same time is more efficient than distant bedrooms needing heat at different times. Ceiling heights may not feel like a climate choice, but low ceilings are more efficient to heat, so there is a place for them. This is why even grand New England homes sometimes have oddly low ceilings. It's the carbon costs of heating the space! In temperate climates, you have more leeway with openness and ceiling heights, but this may change as the climate does. On energy use, there has been a push by sustainability advocates to go all electric on appliances in the home—from heating and cooling units to stoves, water heaters, dryers, and so on—with the thought that electrical grids are becoming far more efficient and source more renewable energies. This is a slow process, but if you have a choice to make, at least this is one metric to consider.

There is constant improvement in the efficiency of home products—windows are better insulated, roofs can be cool, and appliances use less energy. While in another chapter I discuss keeping what you have (see the section "It *is* easy being green), it is prudent to replace older, inefficient features of the home. It will keep you comfortable and keep the energy bills down while also being better for the planet. For example, we were able to update our windows and add insulation to our existing walls and roof when the walls were opened up for structural work. Instead of the inside temperature fluctuating when the weather changes, now our indoor climate stays fairly even, and we save money and energy. It's a magic trick hidden away in our walls. Additionally, we were fortunate that our flat, south-facing roof was a great candidate for solar panels, so most of our energy is produced by them.

Aging in place.

Gone are the days of starter homes where a young couple bought a small home with the thought that they would move on to larger and larger homes with their larger and larger families, until ultimately, they downsized on home size in their retirement years. So many parts of this model are now outdated, from different family structures to availability of real estate. It's just not as realistic these days to sell a house and expect to find another bigger one with all of the stars that need to align to make that work (mortgages, escalating home prices, the stress of moving, selling your current home, jobs, and so on). Now many of us may buy one home, starter or otherwise, and grow and age in place. This is something to consider when looking for your new home. Could you see yourself staying here for the long haul if you had to? Is there space to expand to a second story or convert a basement should you need more space in the future? Is there room in the yard for a second living unit (see the section on "granny flats" in chapter 4) that you or your grown children could move into? Even how the home is laid out can affect how comfortable it will be in your twilight years. In our neighborhood—being in a steep, hilly area—many of the homes have stairs up or down into the main entry. We are lucky to have a street-level entry, but we moved most of the common living areas downstairs in the renovation. This works for us now when we are spry and youthful, but when I watched my aging and increasingly disabled father try to navigate going down the stairs, I saw how essential accessibility is.* Inside the home, we made sure moving through and using the space are as intuitive as possible.

---

*"Universal design" or "design for all" design strategies promote usability of the space for all people—not just you and your family now, but also considering your lifestyle as you age or how your abilities and perception of space change. This includes sensible design we can all appreciate like wide hallways, reachable storage, lower-height fixtures in kitchens and bathrooms, enough space between kitchen counters and islands, showers with seats and without curbs, and so on.

Aging in place also means flexibility in how you use the space. Maybe the office you planned for the first floor can later be repurposed as a bedroom should mobility become an issue. In our home, the space we added at the lower level can also function as a stand-alone apartment. It has a separate entry from the side yard, as well as a kitchen and bathroom. If and when we are empty nesters, we can close off the two levels and create an in-law apartment without too much of a hassle. Considering the future requires some level of fortune-telling—who really knows what will happen? Life tends to get in the way of best-laid plans, but you can at least envision a version of the future where you stay put.

chapter 2

Eureka! You've found it, but it needs some help.

Once you have a place to live, prepare for a project. Also, take some "before" pictures.

Know your land.

Congratulations! You've found a home. Now, find out anything and everything you can about your house. Not only is a bit of research sometimes fascinating, but it's often useful. I found in some old microfiche at the city's planning department that my house originally had an off-street parking space that had since been covered over with a fence. The current zoning rules required that our house have an off-street parking space. With my research, I was able to convince the planner on our project to grandfather that original space in, rather than carve a new garage or carport out of our existing house. That added value to the property without lifting a hammer! There may be interesting tidbits about who built your house and when, and maybe some old permits, so you can find out what was actually done during renovations. Other fantastic resources are your neighbors, especially the older ones. So bake some pies or buy wine in bulk and head on over for a visit. They just might know when the roof was last done, or how the previous owners had the kitchen set up. They probably even have some good gossip about the culture of the neighborhood. I often imagine the widow who lived in our house before us, living simply in this tiny house in the hills for forty-five years. She was a gentle Swiss woman, the matriarch of the street—kind and known to everyone. Many years later, we still get mail addressed to her from the random organizations she supported. Of course, we start fresh creating our own stories when we inhabit a new place, but we can sort of inherit these histories too.

Then, consider getting a property survey. This will be prepared by a licensed civil engineer who uses city-certified data points and your legal property description to determine exactly what you own. When just starting a project, spending several thousand dollars on some metal stakes pounded into the property corners and a piece of paper with some lines on it may not seem the best investment, but it's an important thing to do if you're serious about improving your property, especially with an addition or expansion. Simple things like where your property sits in relation to your neighbors, the street, and fences are included, but bigger issues like utility easements and view restrictions may also be defined, so you can deal with those before you're too far into design. Homeowners often assume the curb or their fences define their property, but this isn't always true, especially in older neighborhoods. Our neighbors' lot was so steep that a tree that used to mark the corner of their property had slid down to our property. Land moves over time, but your property usually doesn't.* Large trees, waterways, or other native species' habitats can also shape your buildable area, and your survey will define this. I worked on one project where there was a jet-fuel pipeline running directly under the property on its way to the Oakland airport—the survey showed its precise location.

The property survey, in many cities, will become critical to home-addition projects because they will be used to figure out specifically how much you can add on. Cities typically have "setback" requirements, which is how far your house needs to be from your property lines. Many older homes don't meet current setback requirements, but not to worry! My house was built ten feet closer to the front setback than would be

*There are cases where your property may be defined by landforms like the centerline or edge of a creek and as such, your property boundary may actually shift over time. This type of property description is not typical, but double-check the legal description.

currently allowed, and I say thank goodness. If we were building today from scratch, we'd have to move the house well into the middle of the lot and we'd be farther from the action on the street. This would be great for somebody wanting respite from public life, but we like being right there. Our survey also showed where one neighbor's fence was on our side of the property line, so when it was rebuilt we made sure it was in the right spot. A few inches here and there don't matter, of course, but it's just good to know where everything lays out.

If you're on a sloping site, especially a steep one like ours, it's essential to also include the topography in the survey. This means more lines on your survey drawing showing elevations of the landforms. Creating those seamless indoor/outdoor transitions will be a snap with accurate slopes. Otherwise, you will either end up with a door to nowhere, or you will spend a lot of time and money moving dirt around to access your yards. We really tried to engage our landscape with our addition. While a realtor or flipper might see that building up a second story (to capture some possible Bay views) rather than building down would have a greater resale value, we wanted to be connected to the land. Luckily, our house on stilts (imagine the proportions of a cigarette pack on its back with eight Virginia Slims holding it up) had almost enough headroom below to not require much excavation—or so we thought: we still had to remove MASSIVE amounts of dirt for the twenty-two, eighteen-inch-diameter concrete piers for the new, earthquake-safe foundation. This dirt was all kept on-site and used to even out some of the treacherous topography of the yard that had sat eroding and sloughing down the hill for the last few decades. The topographical information was essential to making this work.

Some cities also require you to get a geotechnical or soils report. This is a study by a soils engineer that determines what type of soil you have and can help you figure out what type of foundation you need. If you have very sandy soils near an ocean, you will probably need a heavy concrete-slab foundation that can act like an anchored boat on the shifting sands. Claylike and steep soils like ours required deep concrete piers and concrete beams that connected them all together. It wasn't the cheapest foundation, but it was what was required for the area we live in. If your city doesn't ask for a soils report, your structural engineer may. This will allow them to be more targeted in their design. Otherwise, they will make assumptions that are probably a little more cautious than when they know for sure. Small projects or very typical lots won't need this extra expense, but it's good to know these specialists are out there if you need them.

Ideally, our homes could hover just above the ground so we don't disturb the natural landscape and aquifers of the terrain, but, alas, gravity continues to pull us down. Some architecture, like cantilevered homes coming out of a cliffside you see in magazines, livable tree houses, or Fallingwater, the original gravity-defying house by Frank Lloyd Wright, have attempted to defy this force, but in the end, we must usually remain anchored. Until we have lunar neighborhoods and sky-high budgets, the best we can do is to sit gently on the land: minimize movement of soils, adjust the design of the house to what exists, and enjoy the view.

These are the things you can do to prepare for a big project:

- ☐ neighbor visits
- ☐ site survey
- ☐ soils report
- ☐ permit history
- ☐ zoning requirements (see the "Talk to the man" section)

It *is* easy being green!

When considering what you want to do with your home, consider that the greenest thing you can do is to keep what you have. Surely, sustainable design and green building will and should come up more than once when you're thinking of what to do with the house. In fact, it should be a continuous and integral part of the project, in concert with the climate considerations. Designing sustainably is really a whole-house methodology. Efficiency in energy use can span everything from your appliances to windows to lighting to solar panels. While reclaimed wood floors, recycled-content tiles, and locally sourced countertops are all nice elements to consider, don't be fooled that your home-improvement project is not having an impact on the environment. While we installed bamboo floors in our addition, the fact that they were originally harvested in a remote forest and then shipped across a vast ocean kind of diminishes their renewable sourcing. While a material like bamboo is eco-friendly from some metrics, it is not when you look at it from another perspective. All construction projects use ecological and carbon resources, whether it's the electricity used to power all those construction tools or the gas and emissions from your contractor's truck driving back and forth from his home and the lumberyard, not to mention the actual environmental load of your building materials beneath those green surfaces—plywood made with off-gassing glues, termite-treated-wood sill plates, steel shipped across an ocean to support your roof, even drywall and all the gypsum dust that gets released into the air with every screw. Even the concrete required for your foundation has an immense amount of embodied carbon. These construction materials and processes to install them can be designed and specified to minimize waste, greenhouse gas emissions, and toxicity, but keep in mind that the least impact you can have on the environment is to retain as much of the house that you possibly can. While new thermal windows and insulation in your existing house can have a huge positive impact on your energy use, of course the orange shag rug and old wall furnace are better off hauled away. Keeping most of the rest—walls, floors, and roofs— means that much less stuff sitting in a landfill* and that much less newly created embodied carbon.

In our house, we added close to 1,000 square feet, but we also kept the entire 712 square feet of original space. Those skinny redwood posts that once held up the house were kept in place and now sit sanded and finished in our new lower-level living room. We removed sixteen layers of old roofing, which lightened the structural load significantly, then we added insulation, a cool roof,† and eventually solar panels. We broke through the narrow kitchen to make way for the new stairs to

*Some cities require you to recycle or divert as much construction waste as you can from landfills, but this can only be done selectively with certain materials. Your rebar might be recycled, but the drywall isn't. Most of it is going to the dump.

†Cool roofs are literally light-colored or reflective roofing materials designed to reflect heat and sunlight away from your house. If all homes had cool roofs, there would be a collective positive effect on the environment and temperature.

the basement, but otherwise the upstairs is intact, and thus, our dump runs were minimized. To be honest, these decisions to keep most of the house were also made because we needed to maintain a place to live during construction, and it was also cheaper and more efficient in our case. Consider that you may only need to rethink the floor plan, maybe open up some walls to make it more functional. Even radical change can happen within your existing envelope. Better furniture or paint color can help to define and embolden space. Keep or salvage as much as you can, or buy an empty lot.

So what does this mean for you if you are living in a mass-market McMansion that you wish was, well, not? I think our tastes are more nuanced than what is thrown at us in new developments. I refuse to believe what we all actually want is a neighborhood full of homes in various shades of beige. While American culture was founded on the concept of individual freedom and its exuberant expression, this notion has some-how gotten lost in post–WWII homogenous housing devel-opments. Each house is a version of its neighbor, ad infinitum. Even so, I don't recommend tearing these houses down. They are built with tremendous resources, and the answer, short of wholesale rethought of suburbia through densification,* is to renovate. Older neighborhoods that people gravitate to now developed over time. The trees have had time to grow in, creat-ing a shaded streetscape. One neighbor repaints in a bold new color, another adds a second story, and eventually you get the

*There is a nascent movement to eliminate single-family zoning, and this has already started in Minneapolis, with allowing duplexes and quad-plexes in formerly single-family neighborhoods, and in Oregon, which recently eliminated all single-family zoning. California recently instituted state laws allowing more density in single-family neighborhoods statewide. We'll see how this plays out, but I am optimistic!

variety and depth we crave. So get creative with your architect and build on what you have. Going back to my first point that every home has redeeming qualities, I have noticed that these developer homes can be huge. Gone are the days when new developments à la Levittown* featured modest starter homes for newlyweds—these days every developer home features great rooms, nooks, offices, and an abundance of entryway. There is absolutely a way to reconfigure that much space into something more functional, usable, and even glorious.

It is certainly *easier* to build something from scratch. Buying a flat piece of property and putting a building on it is an entirely different proposition. If you want fewer constraints, a brand-new build may be the way to go. The complexity of a thoughtful renovation is more like using a scalpel to craft space out of your existing home. You are finding underutilized space and creating the best relationship of rooms out of what you already have. If you are adding space, you'll need to knit together old and new in a seamless way. There are times when tearing down a home is warranted, such as when you find that no amount of tinkering with the plan is going to work, or the home is in truly terrible shape. A fragmented space is not conducive to modern living, so we should rethink our homes in a holistic, and *whole-istic*, way.

I recently helped a family update their property to align with their current lifestyle and needs, and we realized their house

*Levittown was the first postwar mass housing development featuring compact home design with tiny, identical floor plans. While the concept of providing homes and mortgages to returning WWII veterans and their families was not bad, in practice the subdivisions were highly segregated, by design, and started the trend of homogenous housing that could be built quickly and cheaply. The birth of sprawl.

was deceptively large. They had plenty of space, but the home mostly lacked style and flow. Rooms were divided up and cordoned off from each other rather than allowing spaces (and people) to interact. Views were framed in small windows instead of spectacularly. In this case, a wholesale rethinking of the interior space was the best way to make this house work. We were able to keep the exterior walls and footprint of the home, and by just rearranging the spaces inside the home was transformed.

Talk to the man.

If you are planning a significant remodel—or *any* size addition—I suggest you go personally to the planning or zoning department in your municipality, take them that survey you did or other sketch of your house, and ask about the development requirements. This process varies ever so slightly from place to place, which is why this initial informal consultation is so important.

Typically, you can find out how much you can add on to your house in regard to city-stipulated area limits, setbacks from property lines, height limits to see if you can build up to capture those fabulous views, height restrictions so you don't block your neighbors' views, and so on. These are fairly straightforward. There are also more complex issues in many cities: If your home is already nonconforming to current standards will they let you add on? Are you sitting on a major earthquake fault line or hundred-year flood zone? Ask what documents will be required at submittal for a permit. Soils reports? Design-commission approvals? Local environmental regulations? The powers that be can throw a few wrenches in your plans, so it's best to know early on what you're getting into. I discovered that the mucky sludge at the bottom of our property was technically a protected creek, which required thirty-foot setbacks for new construction. Who knew? The planning department, that's who. Of course your architect can and will do all of this themselves, but a little knowledge never hurts. In case you are thinking that skipping a permit saves costs and hassle (I'm not advising this), it's still a good idea to follow the code, lest a pesky neighbor report you, or your contractor goes rogue. Cities look much more kindly on conforming illegal additions than flagrantly scofflaw ones.

On that note, I've noticed a fear among my friends and neighbors of alerting the city at all about even potential thoughts to improve your home, thinking it will put them on some master list of projects on their radar, but this is simply not true in most cities. The planners are mostly there to help you; they are not secret code-enforcement agents. Most cities do not have the interest in or money for roving officers looking for municipal code violations. Once you've actually applied for a permit, however, there are no guarantees. They may make you take down your illegal fence or legalize your unpermitted in-law unit, so be prepared for some unintended consequences.

While the rules that you have to follow when improving your own property may seem arbitrary, the planning-department guidelines (your city may call it the municipal code, zoning code, or something similar) are there to implement the long-term vision for your particular neighborhood that the city has developed.* Crafting this vision takes years, and it is created with a lot of input, so don't expect it to change readily. The vision could be a traditional suburban neighborhood with stand-alone homes with front yards and hidden garages; it could be a mixed-use area with retail interspersed with offices and residential; it could be more urban, with ground floors dedicated to commercial uses, with housing above. Our local version of the guidelines dictates that our neighborhood is zoned strictly for single-family homes, which means we can't have *even one* corner store in our quasi-rural residential neighborhood, even though it would make the neighborhood more livable and convenient for more residents. Whatever the vision, it is implemented through these planning-code guidelines. What this means for you and your home-improvement project is that you will basically become an agent of change that the city wants to see. If this sounds Orwellian, it's not that sinister. Well, maybe a little. While some municipalities may also weigh in on style with design guidelines for some projects, as well as function and size, your capable architect should be able to maneuver these guidelines with aplomb.

Our permit process went fairly smoothly. For the planning permit, our city planner was appropriately officious and followed all those rules when reviewing our design, some of which we were able to convince her did not apply (they didn't apply, but planners are likely to be very—um—thorough). We live in Berkeley, so of course our fair-minded liberal city wants us to engage neighbors before we even submit an

*Unless you live in a city like Houston, which actually doesn't have zoning, for better or worse. They do have other ways of regulating land use though.

What to ask about at the zoning office:

- ☐ What is the zoning for this address/property?
- ☐ Are there guidelines to _____ (fill in the blank with what you want to do):

  - Add an addition at the (front, side, back)?
  - Add a second- or third-story addition?
  - Dig out a new basement?
  - Add an addition over 500 square feet? Is there a threshold on size?
  - Add an accessory dwelling unit (ADU)?
  - Add a home office?
  - Add a separate building for a rumpus room?
  - Convert part of my home to an office?
  - Convert the garage into living space?

- ☐ What are the limitations on size, setback, and height?
- ☐ Are there specific regulations on the design?
- ☐ What is the zoning process? Does it involve neighbors or public hearings?
- ☐ Do I need an architect?
- ☐ Do I need a survey?
- ☐ What are the submittal requirements?
- ☐ How long does this take?
- ☐ What's next?

---

application to the planning department by posting a giant, bright yellow sign advertising the details of our modest project to all passersby. Thankfully, since the property was in such a deteriorated state, everyone was thrilled to see it get improved. At first. Once concrete trucks blocked the end of the street and contractors took up the already skimpy parking it was a different story. We tried to keep the peace by offering gifts of pottery and candy to the most impacted neighbors, but construction is just a pain, plain and simple. That's why it is important to let everyone nearby know what you're planning and when you're planning it (see chapter 3). Only your own toddler should be waking you up at uncivilized hours, not a jackhammer!

You would hope that cities would have streamlined the permit process so that one approval is all you need, but you're not done yet! Next, you need to get a building permit.* Building codes are developed by an international consortium to decide on things like fire safety, disabled access, structural stability, and energy efficiency. But they could not care less what your house looks like. Your architect will prepare "construction documents" that can also be used for the building permit. This review process is more concerned with minimum standards for safety, not how beautiful or how well designed the house is. They won't judge your tile choices, but they may care about your toilet being low-water use. We submitted a very basic drawing set for the building permit—just the regular, tedious building-code-related stuff like plans, sections, and elevations with structural calculations, window-glazing types, stair dimensions, and setbacks from property lines. Depending on your jurisdiction, the permit reviewer will review the plans to confirm that the house is safe from fire, earthquakes, flooding, and grave personal injury, and that it's energy efficient. I checked in as frequently as possible (before becoming

*Each municipality is different, and I'm describing the typical process in most cities. Check with your local planning or zoning department, or possibly the building department, to confirm the process in your town. Some smaller towns have easier processes, while larger ones are more complicated.

annoying) to stay abreast of the review progress—Was there anything else he needed? Could he e-mail his comments while I was on vacation? Could I come in person to correct anything instead of waiting for official feedback? We wanted to start our foundation before the rainy season, so time was of the essence. We were building our house at a time when the city wasn't inundated with applications for building. Now with my current clients, we usually just have to wait our turn in the queue.

Good neighbors.

People love their neighborhoods because of the neighbors, right? Sometimes. Beyond the good stuff like block parties, watering each other's plants when one of you is on vacation, and general community feelings, there is also friction over trees, fences, dogs, parties, and definitely construction. Change is hard. When we're focusing on the inner workings of our homes, it's easy to lose track of how the project is going to affect the neighborhood. Is your new second story going to block your neighbor's view? If so, is there a way to make less of an impact while still getting a view of your own? Do you have a big new window facing right into your neighbor's bedroom? Even if the design is not an issue, I can tell you now, the neighbors aren't going to like it once it's under construction. There will also be noise and extra traffic. If you live in a townhouse or a flat, the construction may even come right up to your neighbor's walls and floors. Most people are understanding of the necessary-but-temporary nature of the construction process, but it's still a good idea to give people a heads-up on what's going to be happening and when it will be loud or disruptive.

Also keep tabs on your own contractors: Are they parking in the right place? Are they keeping the site clean? Is their music too loud? Essentially, you'll need to manage a lot of expectations internally among your own team and externally with your neighbors.

On a recent in-law unit project in my professional practice, we designed the project to be within the "by-right" guidelines which didn't require neighbor notification, but that didn't mean the neighbors didn't care. Since the neighbors weren't aware of all of the details of the design before construction started, we had a couple of complaints about new windows that would be overlooking adjacent properties. And, once the project was framed up, the impacts became much clearer. In the end, we were able to work with the neighbors on privacy solutions to relieve major concerns, and the resulting project made everyone happy.

Of course owners want to maintain good relationships with the people they'll be living next to for a long time, so these are always difficult conversations to have. Any issues are best resolved in person, preferably at the neighbor's house, so you can see exactly what impacts you are having—and if they are relevant. Sometimes there are easy things you can do to make it better—maybe a paint color, planting something to hide a window, making a deck smaller, or blackout shades to block light. Talk it through, and hopefully people will feel better when their issues are heard.

In urban areas, where most new construction at your neighbor's house is bound to be very close to your own home, there will inevitably be some loss of light or views. In my view, the reason some choose to live in cities is because they appreciate the density. Close proximity is a feature—not a bug—of urban living, and there are ways to mitigate negative relationships as your neighborhood fills in over time.

At my house, I mentioned earlier we were able to reinstate the parking spot that was originally permitted with the house. A neighbor actually complained about this because they feared loss of street parking for the new driveway we restored. We explained we would be the ones parking there anyway and they eventually relented. We didn't increase the height of our house, so shadows and views weren't an issue for anyone. It just goes to show that you never know the concerns neighbors will have until you talk to them about it.

Get an architect—maybe.

My mother-in-law has a pretty negative impression of architects, even though she loves design and both her daughter-in-law and nephew are practicing architects. Her home is an impeccably preserved mission-style home in Southern California, the kind featured in historic home tours. Martha Stewart would bow in reverence to her stacked antique wooden boxes and out-of-print books, accentuated with fresh-cut flowers and twine balls (where does she get those?). However, she feels that her style is categorically out of sync with that of any architect. This all comes from her two encounters with hiring architects herself. One designed the renovation of her bathroom but failed to see that her ceiling could be vaulted up to her roof framing, thereby creating a dramatic, skylight space. The contractor was able to do this once the ceiling was opened up during construction. The other assisted in her family-room addition and didn't initially catch an obscure code requirement, requiring a revision to the original design.

The main job of an architect is to be the homeowner's advocate. They are looking out for your interests in all matters, from design, budgets, and schedules to communicating with contractors and city officials. Maybe my mother-in-law had bad architects, maybe they were good, but I can tell you with certainty that they were not magicians. Their failure was perhaps in not clearly communicating their role. Architects are not time travelers able to figure out exactly how your house was built eighty years ago, or lawyers who read every edition of the ten-volume International Building Code as well as the local municipal codes from cover to cover. They are licensed professionals who are there to guide you through the design process, then through the often-Byzantine permitting process, and ultimately through the construction process. At a minimum, they should have a good understanding of local codes, and a facility with visualizing space. And, perhaps the most quantifiable skill is an ability to draw it all on paper really, really well so that a builder can translate those drawings into a beautiful, livable space.

That being said, every project is different, and I guarantee that even experienced architects see something new with every project. They are learning about your home and your lives as they get to know you. That's why most architects love what they do—there is always something to learn and new ideas to explore. Working with an architect should be a collaborative process, where there is a consistent dialogue and common goals. Some clients have more interest in developing every detail and working through the design, while others are comfortable handing over the reins to a competent designer. If you're in the market, interview many architects and really talk to them, both casually and professionally. Look at their portfolios to see if they, and you, are a good fit. In the end, it may come down to personality—your architect will come to know you pretty well, so choose one with whom you have a good rapport. There are some architects who walk into a space and know exactly what you should do. I call them Mr. (or Ms.) Big Ideas and it's a great skill that exudes confidence in what they are doing. Other architects are more contemplative and will get to know you and the space before jumping into design. And there is everything in between. Consider what is a better fit for you.

So what exactly does an architect actually do, you may ask? Walk into a school of architecture and you may think architecture is adventures in model building, flashy presentations, and zoomy computer fly-through models. On the other hand, ask my father, an engineer, and he'd undoubtedly relate, if not conflate, the architect and the engineer—buildings and bridges, that sort of thing. Most simply put, I think architects are there to support your lifestyle with spatial solutions. Architects bring specificity to your home—yes, probably anyone can design and build a generic space, and you can move into it, but an architect can tailor that space to your most minute needs. From which side of the bed you sleep on to where you park your car or bike or skateboard to how you prepare and eat meals—an architect is there to integrate these daily aspects of life into a seamless existence. Our architecture should make our lives easier, right?

For the most part, architects can have the great ideas for a space, but someone else actually builds those ideas. Gone are the days when the architect was the artisan or when the architect was the engineer. The role of the architect today is something like that of a director in a film project—we have great ideas, but we need the cooperation and talent of others to make that idea work. We are constantly collaborating with the owner (producer), who has the ultimate say in all matters. We incorporate the input of consultants like engineers and specialists (agents, associates) into the architecture. We then rely on the skill and artistry of the builders (cast and crew) to flesh everything out. The process of building your home is a true team effort.

One of the architect's means of communication with clients and contractors and building officials is through technical drawings, which admittedly can be a pretty obtuse creation. In fact, the architect's product can be so vague that it's hard to appreciate the value until you're enjoying your coffee one morning and that soft glow of the eastern sun is lighting up your newspaper. Then you will appreciate your architect. But until then, make sure you understand everything you are shown. Architects may forget that not everyone knows what a parti* is and may need to be reminded to use conventional English. Other means of representation besides flat drawings

*A *parti* is archi-speak for a diagram. Or maybe *diagram* is archi-speak too? All these terms refer to the organizing principal of a design. For instance, a large square flanked by smaller squares may be the parti/diagram for a courtyard home layout. It helps to distill and bring clarity to design concepts, but it doesn't work in all contexts.

could also be used to explain the work—sketches, three-dimensional models (computer models are one way to see space quickly, but an old-fashioned cardboard model may still be the most exciting way to see potential home designs), and tours of similar places are all good ways to really see what you're getting—so don't hesitate to ask for it specifically. Every project is different, even for the architect, and the way the ideas are expressed may need to be adjusted from project to project, client to client.

In the end, sometimes your best option for a simple project may just be—*gasp*—a good contractor. If you are just moving a nonstructural wall, replacing kitchen cabinets, even redoing a bathroom, you don't always need an architect. An architect is really just a middleman when it comes to these types of projects where the owners know exactly what they want, and the contractor can give them just that. And many contractors, if they've been doing this for a while, are actually good designers themselves and can advise on the best path forward. The threshold for needing an architect may be different for every client and contractor, but it can basically be measured by complexity or scope. The more complex or greater the scope of work, the more likely you need an architect. My mother-in-law, with a great sense of her own personal style, can easily make decisions about design elements with a competent contractor, while someone less visual may want something more. There are also competent designers that can help with finishes and layout to guide you through a small project. See what fits best for your needs and personal preferences.

What an architect provides will also vary from project to project and architect to architect. Clarify with your architect what you want—are you looking for design help for the renovation and addition of the spaces in your home down to the level of choosing light fixtures and colors of paint? Or do you want to do that last part yourself? Some clients hire an interior designer in addition to their architect to design finishes as well as furniture and fixtures. Most architects will prefer to design down to the hard architectural surfaces that are attached to the building, including tile and cabinetry, but there is wide latitude here. Early-modern architects like Adolf Loos designed everything from the roof edges and window trim down to built-in couches, carpeting, and door handles in his projects, but that's rare today. And expensive. You'll want to spell this out so you know what you're getting, and what may be additional services and fees. Many of my clients are do-it-yourself types who want to do the work of picking out all of the finishes, while others have literally no idea where to start, and both are fine. Just figure out what you want and find an architect that can work with that.

What to ask potential architects:

Here is a list of fairly open-ended questions to ask potential architects and designers to get the conversation started:

- ☐ What do you like about designing houses?
- ☐ Do you have a portfolio of similar scale and style of project I can look at?
- ☐ How do you work with your clients?
- ☐ Have you designed a project in this city and/or neighborhood before? Were there challenges to that process that you can tell me about?
- ☐ How do you communicate your ideas (drawings, models, digital mediums)?
- ☐ Do you also include the design and specifying of finishes, lighting, and plumbing fixtures?
- ☐ Are you comfortable with letting others design the interiors?
- ☐ What level of detail do you design to? That is, are you also designing built-in cabinetry and trim details?
- ☐ How involved are you during construction?
- ☐ How do you work with contractors?
- ☐ Can you show me some similar projects that you have completed?
- ☐ What is one of your favorite projects that you designed, and why?
- ☐ What about your favorite by another architect?
- ☐ Can you provide references of clients you've worked with before?

These questions may sound like a job interview because that's exactly what it is. See the section "Paper architecture" in chapter 6 for more information on architects, drawings and what to expect.

chapter 3

Getting inspired.

This is when the fun and sometimes overwhelming process of design starts. Time to get a notebook. Or there's probably an app for that now.

Movies instead
of magazines.

Design and lifestyle magazines like *Dwell* and *Wallpaper*,
Pinterest and Houzz boards, or even local real estate list-
ings are a good place to start to get inspired for your new
space, but note that these static images are just one aspect
of space—sometimes you'll see the same prop repositioned
in a new location, or several pictures of the same space from
different angles, making the project look more complex
when it may just be a simple countertop dividing two rooms.
The regular hodgepodge of dishes may get conveniently
replaced with vintage apple-green Russel Wright dinnerware
on picture day. Also, wide-angle lenses make spaces appear
deceptively larger. While most magazines make an extra
effort not to use this space-defying technique, computer
renderings, real estate photos, and other flashy images are
often unrealistic.

There has also been an explosion of home design and décor
Instagram accounts that truly are fun to look at for inspiration.
However, I tend to treat images from design magazines and
Instagram as I do models from *Vogue* and other influencers—
they are stylized visions that have likely been manufactured
and filtered to please you. The actual model (aka space) probably looks like a version of the one in the magazine, just with
more blemishes (clutter) and wearing comfortable clothes
(that couch from your mom's basement). Influencer culture
and design magazines have borrowed a page from fashion
magazines and real estate marketing, offering staged images as
a template to inspire your future stylish life.

There is an inordinate fixation on image-able space, and, admittedly, architects are among the worst offenders. We like to create dramatic and photogenic rooms that we can put in our portfolios and get featured in publications, but sometimes the best space cannot be adequately captured by still camera shots. I can tell you from my own experience that the pictures my professional photographer takes of my projects lend an ethereal quality to the spaces. Most photographers like to take pictures on bright but overcast days to pick up the ambient lighting. This is not to say the homes aren't actually this nice, but the brightness is certainly enhanced, the piles of debris outside a window area are cleverly masked, and angles are maximized for the best take on a space. Power cords and outlets can get mysteriously cleaned up. White rooms tend to be easier to photograph too because you can blow out the color and make anything look bright. Dark rooms with deep tones are harder to capture and need appropriate lighting—I think this is why we don't see many dark rooms in print media. All of this is to say that the professional photograph is one representation of a project. Find others. This is not to dismiss the value and fun of swiping through these images, just take them with a grain of salt. The important thing to remember is that your space should be designed for living, first and foremost. If you are designing for a two-dimensional vignette, part of the spatial ambience is lost. We live in three dimensions, so your space should be considered in such.

Movies are a little better indication of space because stories, as in real life, are the main show. Movies track movement in real time and show space for what it really is: background. It's not the main event. It can assist and enhance, but it is not the focus.

As you move around a room, flat backgrounds morph into dramatic angles, objects in the foreground may momentarily drift across your view, light bounces off of things in different ways from different vantages. The time of day changes how a space looks too. So watch some movies and see what you like. And by movies I don't mean design-y favorites like *Diamonds Are Forever* and *Gattaca*, unless you are designing your own personal lair. I mean regular movies or TV shows. Like *Modern Family* or *Parenthood*. Of course, movies also stylize and fetishize space, featuring dark backgrounds that don't clash with the actor's eyes or some other vague metric. But it's a little more accurate than a still shot. So even better yet, experience some friends' homes that you like and have a conversation about what works. The architecture should almost be invisible in spaces that are really great. All you may notice is comfort, light, and the people you're with.

For me, a certified drafting nerd, the most surefire way of seeing if a space is going to work is to look at a floor plan, which is basically a flattened aerial view of the house if it were sliced horizontally at about three feet high. I know I am biased by being an architect that draws plans for a living, but the plan is at once abstract and subjective. You see all points of view at once—where paths converge, where dead ends stymie, and where relationships can happen. You can quite literally trace your finger along a plan and construct possible narratives as you go. I am probably romanticizing the plan a bit, but it really is the basis of great architecture. Learning to read them is a good skill to have. In fact, reading plans is a lot like reading a novel: the plot is described for you, but your own mind provides the imagery.

Perhaps even more exciting than the plan of your home is the section, which is a vertical slice of your home. It's like opening up a dollhouse and seeing all the floors at once. These section vignettes are sometimes even more telling about openness and unexpected connections than plans—can you yell up to the kids for dinner through a double-height space? I fondly remember a sunken living room where the top of the built-in couch was almost level with the floor above. A simple design move like this can upend what is "floor," what is "seat," and what is "table." Design your sections as carefully as the plan and new, unexpected relationships between spaces emerge. The place where our home's section becomes most interesting is at the back where we have a large deck on the upper level, a smaller deck below, and the backyard below that. The three-tiered effect is really terrific, especially when someone is at each level. Well, maybe not so much when the person above you is holding water balloons, but delightful when they have bubbles. If your home is one story, it doesn't mean you won't be able to consider the section—you can vault the ceilings, put in skylights or high windows, or create lofts to improve the sectional relationships in your home. In medieval churches, the proportional relationship between a tall nave flanked by cozier chapels was a building section that was very carefully and intentionally thought through, with dramatic and iconic results. This is an extreme example of the meaning of *section*, but it illustrates how important height and vertical relation-ships are between spaces. Most homes will feature standard eight-foot ceilings throughout, but if you can pop a ceiling up or create a skylight, it adds complexity and significance to a room.

These plan and section views help shape the cinematic, lived-in narratives that can happen in your home. Most people are looking for the elevation (the drawing of the front façade of your house), and with good reason, since it's something you will look at every day, but that's just one aspect of the space. It's the postcard view, but it's not the life within.

How do you live in your space?

To start thinking about how your home could better support your life, it is essential to figure out the elements of your day: Do you try and hide under your blankets from the glaring eastern sun peeking through drawn curtains every morning, or do you rise gloriously doing sun salutations? Do you like to watch movies in bed, in the living room, on your tablet, at a theater, never? Do you have an elaborate coffee or tea or other beverage ritual? Same for meals—do you eat with family at the dining table, or cozy up in the corner of the couch? Do you cook elaborate dinners, or do you warm up frozen Trader Joe's tamales in the microwave? It's important to be honest with yourself. Maybe it's not ideal to be watching TV while eating dinner, but is it something you would change if you had the proper space? Maybe so. I didn't realize how much I could enjoy cooking until I had a kitchen that was open to the living room. I no longer felt sequestered to a remote place to do "domestic" work. Others have found that some separation of the kitchen allows more concentration and a place to hide. I have also accepted that I only use my bedroom for sleeping, so grand master suites are not really suited to my lifestyle. These types of situations all have spatial implications that should be addressed in your home project. Sometimes your existing space is simply underutilized, and a clever rearrangement can help tremendously, or there are clearly deficiencies to be addressed.

The vision we have of what our homes should look like has to be reconciled with how we actually live. It seems like everyone on HGTV "loves to entertain" and "has frequent guests." Is that true? I just can't believe that every person has such an active social life, but maybe I'm sheltered, or the HGTV crowd self-selects the social ones. Or I just don't get invited out much. But even my most social friends have people over maybe two or three times a month. Yes, we want to be able to entertain with cocktail parties and elaborate Thanksgivings, but we also need to accommodate three meals of our own every single day. And laundry. And baths. And other general drudgery. If we design for everyday instead of only those special days, our houses will be comfortable for daily life and we'll be emotionally ready for the real holidays.

There are obvious spatial needs you will have, like space for a certain number of beds and baths, a home office to work from home or do household management, formal rooms if you're so inclined, but it's important to consider these concrete needs as a part of the flow of your everyday life, not as checkboxes on a list. It's not just about the room, but how you will use it. You may have kids that need their own rooms, but do you want them close by, or do you want them down the hall and around the corner? If kids share a room, how can it be designed for both privacy and community? Do you live with extended family, and do you like them? Is yours that house where all of the neighbor kids hang out? Do you want it to be? These are all issues that can affect your architecture—and involve issues of privacy, lighting, and access—in other words, your lifestyle. You can begin to rethink what these spaces really are. A bedroom can literally be just that—a room with a bed, but it could be so much more if that's your thing. It could open up to a sibling's room with a simple sliding door. It could have its own outside access and en suite kitchenette for a studio-like feel. It could be a glorified closet, if you so desire. I just saw an old house built in the 1950s for a large family, and the kids' bedroom was literally laid out like an army bunker, with identical built-in closets dividing the rooms and Dutch doors facing a shared pseudo-mess hall. It worked for them, apparently, since it has survived for almost seventy-five years!

Similarly, bathrooms can expand or contract or contort to meet the specific needs of your lifestyle—we've done a few bathrooms where the shower and the sink areas are separate but connected with a door, and each area can also be accessed separately. This way, people who share a bathroom can use different parts of it without discomfort. Soaking tubs seem to be getting more and more luxurious every time I turn around, so they basically need their own room. My first flat in San Francisco had the toilet in a separate room from the tub and sink. I don't know the history there, but it seemed very Victorian since people so prized their prudence and modesty in that era. To address some spatial limitations, a bathroom in my house was intended to be both a master bathroom as well as the guest bathroom, so there are two doors—one from the hallway and one from the bedroom. This ended up being over-kill. We didn't really need two ways into a small room after all!

In my home, I was very intent on having the kitchen look out onto our backyard canyon. I had visions of the kids playing back there, while I could be up in the house and still keep an eye on them. This meant I had to sacrifice the office/guest room having that view, but it was a trade I was willing to make since the time I spend in the office room is pretty focused—the view out would have been wasted. So feel free to rethink all of these notions in your own home. You are making it yours, after all. Sometimes we do just need a room of our own.

Your architect probably has a list of questions they'll ask you when starting design, but here are a few things to consider when figuring out what your spatial needs are. Don't worry if this is too specific. It's just a way to start thinking about what is actually essential. I would consider each of these in relation to filters of privacy, lighting, and access. For example, does a particular space need to be private, does it need natural or artificial lighting, and does it need access to the outdoors or another room?

The days of your life:

What do you do when you wake up?

- ☐ Eat breakfast—you'll need a space to prepare meals and eat
- ☐ Make coffee—whether it's an elaborate ritual with espresso machine and frother, or Mr. Coffee, you'll need a place for this
- ☐ Do yoga/workout—where does this need to happen?
- ☐ Shower—do you need to be able to use the shower at the same time as someone else brushing his or her teeth?

Do you leave the house to work?

- ☐ Yes—skip to next question.
- ☐ No—do you need a separate home office, or will a desk in the corner suffice? Do you need a separate entrance for clients, or just a sense of autonomy?
- ☐ Sometimes—same as above.

If you have kids, what do they do all day?

- ☐ Go to school—hurrah, the house is empty!
- ☐ Stay home—lots of spatial needs for play, sleep, eating, and so on, but most of these overlap with regular needs.
- ☐ Stay home and you also work at home? Then separation of spaces will need to be considered.

What do you do at night?

- ☐ Cook dinner—you'll need adequate kitchen and dining space.
- ☐ Get takeout—you'll still need room to eat and throw away the garbage.
- ☐ Do homework—will this be in the bedroom, or in a shared space?
- ☐ Watch movies—do you want a separate room for media or the same as regular living room?
- ☐ Read books—do you need a cozy nook, or do you read in bed, or in a bath?

Sleeping

- ☐ How many different beds do you need?
- ☐ Who can share?
- ☐ Do you and your partner need separate spaces for different bedtimes or wake times?
- ☐ Do you need natural light to wake up?

Bathing

- ☐ What is your bathing ritual—daily morning shower/luxurious evening bath?
- ☐ Bathroom products—I'll let you consider all of your typical toiletries and storage needs since everyone has a specific routine here.

Storing your stuff

- ☐ Pantry—bulk storage needs and/or daily groceries?
- ☐ Clothes—walk-in closet or a small wardrobe and dresser?
- ☐ Books—do you have a library or prefer not to keep books after you've read them? Same for the kiddos.
- ☐ Other—we all have many other things to store, from bikes to camping gear, crafting materials to holiday needs.

Entertaining style

- ☐ None—you prefer to keep your home your private sanctuary.
- ☐ You have couples over occasionally.
- ☐ You have big parties on many occasions, and neighbors are walking in and out.
- ☐ You just host Thanksgiving.
- ☐ Holidays—is it very important to you to feature the Christmas tree in a prominent spot every year? It may sound silly, but this is actually a big deal for a lot of people!

This is just a teaser to get you thinking about what you must have and want to have, and to see how your simple daily tasks need certain physical spaces to work best. For a few days, be hyperconscious of how your day goes. Are you always dropping your bag by the front door because there is nowhere else to put it? Do you need to keep your shades drawn for the privacy because your windows look right out onto the street? You are certainly already aware of these daily nuisances, but many of these issues can have a designed response. And the answer to many needs may just be a traditional home; after all, homes were developed over time to adapt to life inside, but it's good to think it through.

Style.

There is a lot of focus in real estate about style—homes can be Queen Anne, colonial, craftsman, ranch, midcentury modern, or the catchall "contemporary." All of these "styles" conjure up images of what the house looks like (maybe it has a gabled roof and deep eaves, or perhaps there is a fireplace and stone hearth, or a picket fence marches around the perimeter of the front yard), but I think they can also define certain lifestyles. We should remember that certain architectural customs were developed for specific locations and particular cultures. Pitched roofs are much better at shedding snow than flat ones, so your alpine home should definitely have one. Victorian-era homes developed a network of hallways so that servants could discreetly come in and out of rooms without being seen, but that is not a feature that is relevant in modern households.

When you start thinking about your home-improvement project, certainly style will be near the top of your list of considerations. These days everyone seems to be tearing down the walls in their homes to create open floor plans, because our lives are more communal, with overlapping uses. Before, we would cook in the kitchen, bring the meal to the dining room, then retire to the living room (or salon?). Now, all of these uses are less clearly defined—everyone can help cook, and we can eat around a kitchen island or on the couch rather than in a separate room. The open plan* is an architectural response to shifting lifestyles. This is what home improvement is all about. How can you update the essential qualities of your home to work better with how you actually live?

When you change the interior of a home to be more conducive to today's world, there are a few strategies to take. To consider a home's history, whether it's the period custom detailing or the arrangement of rooms, you can radically alter the home to create a modern interior while preserving the exterior. You often see this in old brownstones and Victorians that have essentially been gutted, resulting in an airy and bright interior space, yet the façades are intact. Or you can make more subtle adjustments in the style of the original, preserving what you can but making it work for you today. I suggest that you not be a slave to the style of the home unless it's truly a unique example of a particular style of architecture and its loss would be deeply felt, and let your

*I read a study that looked into the phenomena of forgetting what you meant to do when you're in the middle of walking through the house to do it. It found that walking through a portal of some sort—either a door or some similar transition—actually caused participants to have these common memory lapses. Do open plans help us remember better?

needs guide the design. It's an aesthetic style, not an ethos for living.

Where the façade isn't a precious historic resource with untouchable details, a façade renovation is a good opportunity to align the interior of the home with the exterior. In my professional practice, an older home had undergone a massive renovation in the last gasp (circa 1987) of the postmodern era resulting in a thoroughly pomo* exterior, complete with fake turrets and spade and club motifs throughout. This exterior contrasted with the fairly modern, well-laid-out interior. We took this opportunity to create a new light-filled entry that more closely aligned with the interior and eliminated the Jekyll and Hyde character of the home. It's all Hyde now.

A home today is the space you need to fulfill both your family's daily needs and your long-term goals, no matter the trim detail around the windows. We've grown accustomed to things like bay windows and crown molding as signifiers of home, and a nice home at that. However, let's take a step back and remove these notions of what a home should be, and instead focus on what we need to make our lives run smoothly and beautifully. This begins with the layout of spaces, from the entryway through the living, working, and sleeping spaces, and to the outdoors and how these all connect to each other. Style will follow the use—this is sort of a version of form

---

*Pomo, short for postmodern, refers to an architectural style that was a backlash to the austerity of postwar modernism. It was often playful and nonsensical, resulting in odd, noticeable shapes signifying "this is architecture."

follows function*—but it doesn't mean there is *no* style. Design style develops along with the design of space.

Our home, when we bought it, certainly had a style—it was literally midcentury modern, built it 1954 in the style of the day. It essentially followed the rules of earlier modernism espoused during that time (see footnote, page 9). Prominent early modernists promoted precision in detail and materials, and expansion of interior space to the outdoors. There was a lot of talk about purity and truth, which was perfectly relevant in the burgeoning new era of enlightenment in architecture and art. The title of a book on modernism, *Ornament Is Crime*, sums up the sentiment.

Under these guidelines, our unimproved home was almost complete when we bought it—we'd only need to throw some lawn chairs and a planter on the roof to create a roof deck and we'd be golden. But the home did not meet our specific needs, nor address the beautiful site as artfully and conveniently as we would have liked, so we departed from the frigid rules of modernism and created our own as we went. Today's modernism has evolved, but many of its original features remain—horizontality, lots of glass, clean details. These are all fine and noble features, many of which I've integrated into my own home, but even as a modern architect, I find these stylistic conventions too systematic and stifling. The most modern thing we can do is break the rules, right?

*Early Chicago architect Louis Sullivan coined a version of this phrase when designing the city's first iconic skyscrapers. It meant the modern use of structural systems, which seems to imply the resulting design would just be a series of concrete floor plates held up with steel, then clad with whatever efficient material, but in reality, Sullivan developed highly articulated iconic buildings. Style emerged.

The point I'm trying to make about style is that it is at best fleeting, at worst irrelevant. Style evolves, so you don't need to be a slave to it. You can define it as you go. Anything you do today, with modern materials and modern methods, is by definition modern. If modernism was about abandoning the hierarchical, patriarchal society of years past in favor of democracy and egalitarianism, why muck it up with new rules for this revolution? Rules leave little room for whimsy and taste. I don't believe in picking a look for a home and trying to design within that narrow framework. Instead, begin with the inside/outside functions of your home and go from there. The style will develop naturally. Windows need to be where they will provide light, air, and views, roofs sometimes need to overhang for shade, walls define certain spaces. Of course, finessing all of this into a cohesive whole takes creative skill, and that's where you and your architect can develop your own personal style.

Nonscientific questionnaire to determine your personal style:

Which of these artists appeal to you?

☐ Mondrian
☐ Monet
☐ Frank Stella
☐ Manet
☐ Andy Warhol
☐ Banksy
☐ Jenny Holzer
☐ Clementine Hunter

Of the following, which is your favorite city or place?

☐ Amsterdam
☐ Denmark
☐ New York, NY
☐ Polynesia
☐ Los Angeles, CA
☐ Columbus, OH
☐ San Francisco, CA
☐ Just like, the woods

Who is your style icon?

☐ Calvin Klein
☐ Martha Stewart
☐ I'm hip, with it, and dress like a YouTuber
☐ Sidney Poitier
☐ Lady Gaga
☐ My mother
☐ Janelle Monáe
☐ Janice Joplin

What's your favorite drink?

☐ Water
☐ Water with cucumber
☐ Dragon drink
☐ Whiskey sour
☐ Passionfruit La Croix
☐ Absinthe (or specialty cocktail)
☐ New Coke
☐ Sun tea

What's your favorite emoticon? (trust me, this is a very precise process)

☐ :| ☐ B)
☐ :)   ☐ :O
☐ :D   ☐ >:)
☐ :*   ☐ ;)

What's your favorite music?

☐ Classical *and* death metal
☐ Jazz
☐ Pop and sometimes also garage rock
☐ German hip-hop, mostly; international music
☐ Indie
☐ Folktronica, baroque pop, Celtic New-Age type stuff
☐ It's kind of hard to explain, but I guess a blend between dark gothic trap, rap, and Brit-pop
☐ My own cover band—we do mostly Fleetwood Mac

What's your home-style icon?

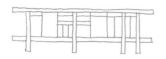

A. Farnsworth house

B. Eames house

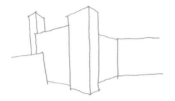

C. Casa Barragán

D. Spanish villa

E. Alan-Voo family house

F. New Orleans shotgun house

G. Victorian house with modern interior & a roof deck

H. Beach palapa

If you chose:

mostly A—you have a modern aesthetic, and prefer clean lines, hard surfaces, and neutral colors

mostly B—you are somewhat modern, but also like natural materials and soft colors

mostly C—you are a free spirit who likes bold colors and supergraphics

mostly D—you have a classic, international style and are drawn to other cultures

mostly E—you are stylish and like to keep abreast of the new and cutting edge

mostly F—even though this sounds like a bad report card, this actually means that you are thoughtful, and intentional about design preferring the local and handmade

mostly G—you like to think outside the box

mostly H—you are more traditional, with a folksy edge

a fairly even spread—you're pretty normal. Congrats!

Personally, I am a CCGDHHB, so clearly I am modern yet traditional/folksy! It just goes to show that most of us probably have eclectic tastes and can't be so easily defined.

Design is (relatively) cheap.

Designing your home is a lot like being pregnant—you'll get lots of unsolicited advice, there are millions of online and paper resources espousing contradictory theories, and, inevitably, someone will want to pet your belly. Well, maybe not actually pet your belly, but people do have a lot of advice from their own experiences with renovations. When you're working with your architect or designer, it may feel like you are setting your money on fire while you try to land on a final design, but honestly, this is the best time to experiment with ideas— before it's under construction and much harder and more expensive to change. It's still just paper, yet to be realized.

During the design process, you and your architect may think you've stumbled upon "the one." This design has it all, it seems. It has grace, it has grandeur, it makes your heart go pitter-patter. Those sexy computer renderings make it look like the life you've always wanted. Look at you, throwing parties while your kids play peacefully in the corner! That's so-o-o you! But before jumping ahead at this point, it would behoove you to look at a completely different scheme. You can't change things once they're built, so the design phase is the one chance you have to look at another option.

Even we architects can get seduced by our own internal processes and drawings, and we tend to gloss over some of the glitches in a design. The process itself can get too precious. It helps to take a step back and look at another equally workable option because it brings the problems of each design to the surface so that they can be dealt with. You will probably stick to the original concept, but you'll likely come up with some tweaks that borrow from another idea too.

In our home, we planned on staying in the house through construction as much as possible, so our options were fairly limited if we were to keep some livable area intact. We designed an addition that could slide under our existing floor level, keeping the upper level untouched. While a word like *slide* is one of those words an architect would use, as if construction were simple Jenga blocks that get pulled in and out as needed, the reality was that nothing in our construction "slid" except the mud down our hillside. We definitely looked at more tumultuous options, like one contractor who suggested that we move the entire house into the street so we could do the work below. Hmmm. Interesting notion. That idea was obviously tabled because we were already walking a narrow path with neighbors and putting our house in the street was not going to help matters. But it was intriguing. We realized that we didn't have to think of our house as a fixed entity. Since we were ripping it from its foundation anyway, we had some leeway in how it was repositioned. We could lift the house a few feet to capture a little more view, get a little more basement. Or move it back to get more front yard. But alas, this idea came too late in the process—we had already begun construction. We should have explored these options when it was all just paper and models.

One idea that finally gained traction during design was the issue of our bedroom. Our floor plan for a lower-level addition basically worked, but we kept trying to shoehorn our future bedroom into the back corner of the house, ignoring the problems with that idea, one being that the room would not get much light, and the other being that we would be on a separate floor from our still-too-small kids. We had become so intent on leaving the upstairs alone that we initially overlooked the obvious solution of creating the bedroom there. We briefly looked at doing an upstairs addition rather than a lower one, from which we finally sifted out this bedroom idea. Having the bedroom upstairs also created a better diagram for the house—bedrooms/quiet upstairs, living room/loud downstairs. The only drawback was that we would not have a place upstairs (the floor you enter the house from) to receive guests—you immediately go downstairs when walking in. Kind of weird, I suppose? But this was our house and we made it work, and no one has ever complained. At least not to our faces. Now we have nice sunny bedrooms, and our living space is cozy and opens to the yard.

Simpler design options should also be investigated while it's all still paper. On a recent project where we opened up a kitchen, we decided to flip the direction of the seating counter late in design. It was a small change design-wise, but it made the kitchen feel more like an intentional space instead of a thoroughfare. It was also a change that was almost imperceptible in drawing format, so make sure you understand what you are being shown by your design team. It never hurts to ask for clarification or more information so that you get what you want.

chapter 4

Designing for your life.

Be specific and be authentic when working with your design team.

Entranced.

The first thing you interact with when coming to a home, whether you're in a high-rise condo, a townhome or brownstone attached to many others, or a stand-alone home, is the front door. The door itself is the physical thing you interact with. It's pretty much a given you will have one. (I haven't seen the front door get "disrupted" yet, though I'm sure they're working on it in Silicon Valley.) The door is the separation between inside and outside, private and public, home and town, and you'll need to create a sense of transition for a welcoming and comfortable space. How this transition is designed can be an entire exercise in and of itself. Is there a long meandering path between the sidewalk and the door, which can create a sense of separation? Or if it's close to the street or sidewalk, maybe a simple awning provides cover from the elements, and a soft porch light gives a warm glow. You may not have the freedom to change your apartment entry, but small moves like the door hardware and color, or even a new doormat, can create a warm welcome. I like to set the tone of the home with this outdoor approach—is it a serene, quiet space or is it an exuberant home? Some of the personality of the home can come through before you even open the door.

Luckily, our front door faces south, so it's a naturally sunny spot where we tend to want to bask. However, there isn't a sidewalk along the street, so people have to step abruptly off the narrow street to approach the house. In designing the entry sequence from street to door, we wanted to slow the pace of visitors and create a space in front of the front door. We added a new gate with an old-fashioned ringing bell, signifying where you enter the property. Next, you walk across stepping-stones to an arbor across a front deck teeming with vining plants. On nice days, guests don't need to go any further than this transitional outdoor "room," because it's a comfortable space to stop and chat.

To design for your outdoor-to-indoor transition, think about what you do when you arrive to your neighborhood by bike, car, or bus, get to your street, and then walk through the door. How long is that process? You want to look forward to coming home, and you want your guests to enjoy coming over. I don't necessarily think you need a clearly marked entry—maybe you want something discreet so it's not so prominent from the public way. The landscaping and hardscape can help to define paths so people know they're on the right one. The front door could be the main design feature of the outside of the home, which is a fairly traditional and useful design concept. I think clues about where the front door is are helpful—I've definitely arrived at homes where I'm not sure if I'm knocking on the front door or a patio door—but this is a personal choice. I'm just saying you should think about it. How does the entry to your home align with how you want to enter it? On a busy street in San Francisco, we redesigned a home's entry to be off the side yard through a gate rather than off the front. It afforded the family privacy and limited solicitors knocking on the door at all hours.

Once you cross the threshold, as important as the outdoor sequence to the door is having a place to put your stuff when you shut the door behind you. Nothing clutters up the view from the front door more than the crush of jackets, shoes, lunch boxes, and backpacks that necessarily enter the house, but get stranded at the first available open space. The solution is to make this space intentional. A coat closet is the old-school solution where you can shove everything out of sight, but this never worked for my family. Hangers are too high and awkward for kids, shoes get trampled and pushed around, and it was just too dark. Inevitably, things get lost in the shuffle until you do an annual clean-out and rediscover those soccer cleats you thought were lost in the fields! The older-school (like colonial era) solution is the mudroom. The mudroom is an intermediate space that isn't quite inside, but it's definitely not outside, where you can sit and take off your muddy shoes, hang your bags and jackets on hooks or hangers, and be on your way. It's like a southern porch, but more geared toward inclement weather. Back in the day, the mudroom was usually a back entrance, or the equivalent of the garage entrance to the house. It was primarily for the residents of the house, while guests were received through a more formal front entry.

Presumably, guests were not expected to take off their shoes back then, as is increasingly common these days, so the mud-room is an excellent adaptation of an old solution to a modern quandary. There have been studies that tracking all of those street and sidewalk germs into the house isn't great for interior environment. On the other hand, there have also been studies that find we don't have enough germs in our new hermetically sealed homes. So, the verdict is still out, I suppose. But a place to stop and prepare yourself for coming in the home is a good thing. Mentally, we can file this entry space away as a blip in the entry sequence. You really enter the house proper after this ancillary space. Also, an intermediate space, like a foyer or

Items you have with you when you walk in the door:

	Hook?	Hanger?	Bin?	Y/N	Daily?	Weekly?	Seasonally?
	CAN IT GO ON/IN A:			CAN IT BE SEEN?	DO YOU USE IT:		
Keys							
Purse							
Jackets							
Sports gear							
Shoes							
Wallets							
Dog leash/gear							
Mail							
Tote/grocery bags							

mudroom, provides a sense of entry to a home. There's nothing more jarring than walking directly into someone's living room, both for the person sitting there watching *Friday Night Lights*, or in some awkward yoga pose (or both), and for the one walking in. Of course, now I sound like I'm getting elaborate, talking mudrooms and foyers, but gracious entry can be achieved by simpler means, like a simple step up or down, or a partial wall that divides the entry from the home proper. Either way, you are giving yourself and your guests a moment to take a breath before entering the fray.

What happens next? Does everyone retreat to a bedroom? Or are people coming home at dinnertime, so they need to wash up and sit down right away? This will inform how much space you need. If you're going to your rooms anyway, maybe all the stuff that comes with you can also go there, keeping the entry fairly clean. If not, what do you need to store in your mudroom? I like to qualify these items in terms of how they need to be stored, and if they can be seen or not. Then you can develop a great, specific solution for your home. The chart on the previous page can help you sort out the particulars.

Everyday kitchens.

IMHO, flawless, gleaming kitchens are overrated. Mark Bittman, the renowned chef and author of bestselling cookbooks and the former *New York Times* food column The Minimalist, shocked his readers when he published a picture of himself cooking in his tiny non-trendy kitchen. He had Formica countertops, hardly any counter space, and off-the-shelf cabinets. Yet his turkey breast turned out juicy and delicious. Similarly, I saw that Michael Pollan, author of *The Omnivore's Dilemma*, was renting his home out in my town, and his kitchen was perfectly practical. My mother—a fantastic albeit less well-known cook who can whip a great meal out of eggs and ketchup (MacGyver-style!)—also has a pretty minimal kitchen in her urban condo, consisting of about eighteen inches of tiled countertop and the minimum of requisite appliances. Yet she manages to make minced chutneys and filleted salmon curries to die for. My good friend Melinda basically grew up in her parents' restaurant and is now a global food and wine critic, yet I can attest her tiny Tokyo flat does not have a Viking range.

The point is you don't need a great kitchen to be a great cook. It would be nice to have a chef's dream kitchen, whatever that means to you, but kitchens are one of the most expensive elements in any home project. Besides the equipment itself, there are so many finishes to consider (and buy), from backsplashes to countertops to hardware and cabinets. Even the lighting for kitchens costs more. In the 1990s and 2000s, granite kitchen counters with stainless steel appliances were the Corian surfaces and lacquered black of the 1980s, which themselves were the Formica and lime green of the 1970s. Just ten years ago, we were doing Carrara marble with natural wood. Now, all of a sudden, it's quartz countertops with painted white cabinets. Who knows where things are headed, but by the time this book is published, I suspect color will be back. Commercial-style stainless steel kitchens have become trendy among the more adventurous set, but note that stainless steel is used in restaurants for its sanitary properties, not its ease of use. It's cold and easily scratched. In other words, kitchen designs are fads that change frequently, so don't feel obligated to install the latest kitchen craze in your home.

My advice is to create a kitchen that works for *you*. Perhaps more important than the look of a kitchen is its functionality and proximity to other parts of your house. We tend to cook while we are also doing something else these days—watching the news, supervising the kids, socializing. Perhaps it needs to be open to the living room so you can keep an eye on things and talk to your guests, with open shelving so you can find your stuff easily. Perhaps you tend to leave your kitchen a mess and would like it best hidden yet accessible. It needs to be practical for your cooking and living style. Clients often *expect* to spend tens of thousands of dollars on a new kitchen without even putting pen to paper, just because that's what they've been told, but you can get a great kitchen affordably and conscientiously. You can even create an excellent beautiful kitchen with freestanding pieces, rather than a custom, shop-built cabinet system. Or you can splurge on appliances but get prefab (or in the case of IKEA—*you-fab*) cabinets. A fully custom cabinet system can be an expense that doesn't always pay off, unless you have very specific needs about joinery and hardware. Some practical issues like having a functional relationship between your workspaces and appliances and sink should be carefully considered, but I think we should stop treating the kitchen like a showpiece. It's a room, where we regularly make huge messes. It should be somewhat aspirational: cooking would definitely be easier and more enjoyable if you have a better kitchen space, but if you hate cooking now, a new kitchen will not radically change you.

I'm not saying that we revert to the old-fashioned kitchens off of the back of the house; cooking and eating today are such integral and communal parts of modern life. But there is something to be said for simplicity. So invest in some good knives and a sturdy dining table and leave the kitchen light-filled and functional. When we first built our kitchen, we started with stand-alone furniture pieces we had accumulated for countertops and storage, and a walnut sink cabinet built by my husband. When we finally put in our "forever" kitchen, we matched the warm walnut and used dark soapstone for the countertops. It turns out soapstone is a very tolerant material that develops a patina with age, which works well with our kitchen skills.

What's Your Proportion?

We can all identify these essential kitchen elements no matter your cooking style. What type of home cook are you?

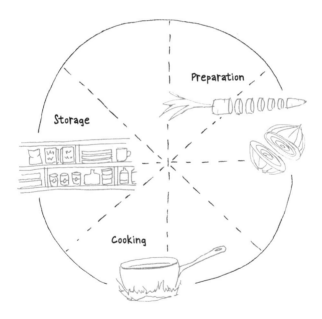

While I'm on the topic of kitchens, my very favorite kitchen I've seen lately is not from the latest Poggenpohl showroom (precision German engineering for kitchens—if you want a kitchen that looks like a glittering laboratory, this is your place!), but on PBS: it's the servants' kitchen on *Downton Abbey*. Once you're done snickering, notice that their kitchen is beautiful and elegant. It is an L-shaped kitchen with ovens and storage along the sides and a long wide farm table in the middle that serves as meal prep and dining space for the servants. The only thing I would change is that the servants wouldn't be slaving away for an aristocracy. This is a fantasy kitchen as much as any other, but it illustrates functionality *as* beauty. Similarly the main residence in *The Handmaid's Tale* also has a lovely working kitchen. What is it about dystopian reality's kitchen designers?

All this being said, I do believe strongly in built-in cabinets elsewhere in the house—bookshelves, benches, closets, pantries. Kitchens get replaced, but built-ins are forever. I think I'll embroider this on a pillow. For kitchen design, I like to keep things simple with a trio of priorities and relationships for a functional kitchen. The proportions of areas for preparation, cooking, and storage will vary depending on your cooking style.

But what does each of these mean to you? For an eager baker, you may need marble prep surfaces and double ovens, and lots of storage space for various pie and cake pans. An avid Costco shopper is going to need lots of cold and room-temperature storage. A slow-food aficionado may need lots of prep space, but less deep storage. Think through each of these elements to determine what you really need in your kitchen.

Nurture nature.

The San Francisco Bay Area, where the weather is never quite sweltering, nor is it ever freezing, is a pretty nice place to live. San Francisco has even been called the air-conditioned city for its reliable 68-degree temperatures. We do have to endure gloomy overcast mornings to earn some late morning sunshine, after which we pile on the hoodies and scarves as the cool evening fog rolls in. From November to March, you can count on some prolonged days, if not weeks, of solid drizzle. The rain never becomes a true cathartic thunderstorm with dramatic lightning and washed-out roads that I remember from my childhood in more tropical locations, nor are these rainy days akin to a cleansing spring shower, with happy rainbows emerging afterward. No, these NorCal storms are more subtle and relentlessly even keeled. As bleak as the drizzle can be for sun lovers, they do serve a purpose—they drench and give life to the bounty of gardens in this plant-loving zone.

Because of this temperate climate, we can have almost year-round access to the outdoors, so it was important to make that possible in our own home. Many homes in our town have amazing and diverse landscapes surrounding them, from ebullient succulents to whispering grasses, as well as the attendant deer and wild turkeys. However, the homes themselves can feel hemmed in by awkward access to these oases, especially older homes that were built before the 1950s. The '50s saw the advent of an emphasis on easy indoor-outdoor connections. This connection is why some people are so gaga over midcentury modern—it's not just the Danish teak furniture, it's the connection with nature. Before that time, homes were designed to act as frames for the view, and homes were still seen as a respite and protection from the elements, with little true engagement with the outdoors.

Seeing clear through a house from one end to the other and beyond through transparent, barely-there glass is an amazingly tranquil experience. Large panes of glass with almost invisible frames truly bring the outdoors in, while windows with thick frames tend to demarcate indoor from outdoor, making them separate realms. Wood framed windows can create a cozy space where your view is like a framed picture rather than where you are at that moment. Window size can also have similar impacts on the feeling of openness and connection— small punctuated windows will feel different than oversized expanses of window walls. Your approach to the view will help you decide on how to approach the design of windows and glass (see the next section for more on windows). Likewise, an old-fashioned side kitchen door may be great for taking out the trash, but it leaves something to be desired for today's world if you are looking for a seamless transition to the outdoors. An incidental side door, while useful, is just about pure efficiency rather than an intentional, designed way to enjoy the outdoors that is integrated with how you live. Considering your particular climate, make seeing and getting out easy and unbroken. Even snowstorms have their charm when viewed (through insulated glass) from a cozy fireplace.

Solar orientation plays a major role in outdoor access. You will always be drawn to the sunny side of your home if you live in a temperate-to-cool climate, or the shady side in an arid-to-hot one. Accept that side of your home as the one you will use most, so make it comfortable to do so. We have a hundred-foot-long north-facing backyard, and a twelve-foot-long south-facing front yard. Guess which gets used more? Our tiny front area has been maximized for all possible uses—an intense succulent and moss garden,* a linear deck for riding scooters and playing, a wood trellis that also provides support to trumpet vines and hops, potted plants, and seating all enliven the sunny days we spend there. There is about a month in the summer when we can comfortably enjoy our other deck on the north side as the sun peeks over the top of our house, and it is lovely indeed. The rest of the year? Not so much. It tends to receive the brunt of the winds whipping up the canyon. The house, even with its low-slung roof, blocks the southern sun for most of the year.

The backyard has remained mostly wild. A makeshift fire pit, hammock, and rope swing are the main improvements there. And so far, we still like the deer and watching their seasonal changes from fawn to doe or buck. I still throw past-prime apples into the yard for them. I may change my mind when a mountain lion or bobcat pops into the yard, but that hasn't happened yet. The sun, the views, and a way to get to both are the keys to a home integrated with the surroundings.

Light it up.

To take advantage of the solar orientation of your home, place glazed openings like windows and sliding doors strategically. A picture window in your breakfast nook may be nice, but it would be spectacular if it's facing east, capturing the sunrise.

*Strangely, both types of plants can thrive in our Northern California temperate climate!

On the other hand, west-facing windows can be almost too bright and cause unbearable glare in the afternoon. Awnings or adjustable shades are practically essential. In coastal California, these western windows are a catch-22; on the one hand you can't shut out those gorgeous Pacific sunsets, but on the other hand, the heat and glare from 4:00 to 6:00 p.m. are almost too much to handle. Eastern windows bring the sunrise. Northern windows bring a subtle, indirect light, while southern sun can be pleasant in the winter, yet oppressive in the summer. If you are hemmed in by neighbors, consider the roof your fifth solar orientation and create skylights. Use these orientations of natural light to craft your home. One project I remember from architecture school created apertures so precisely positioned that a single ray of light beamed onto your dinner plate on your birthday. A nifty harnessing of the sun's power, I must say. If you strategize these solar aspects, you can create a home that will hardly need to use artificial lights during the day.

Our property's entrance to the street faces south, with a backyard canyon facing north. This orientation gave us the perfect opportunity to really open up the back wall with lots of windows, glass doors, and decks. It's private from neighbors and street views, and there is no direct sun, so we don't need shades or curtains at all. The west side was a little more complicated. There was an existing huge horizontal window in the former living room and soon-to-be-bedroom that must have had a view of the Golden Gate before the neighbor's house was developed (darn!). We had already experienced the searing rays of light that came in the afternoons, but since this would be a bedroom now, where we only slept and read late at night, we decided to just replace the old single-pane window with a new efficient one of the same size. We still get great ambient light in the morning, but only our houseplants are there to receive the intense afternoon sun. Downstairs, our kitchen had a west-facing wall, so I definitely didn't want the brightest sun right when I was likely to be cooking as the sun was setting. We placed high windows above shelves so the kitchen is bright and naturally illuminated, but the sun's rays go over our heads. The south wall contains the front door and stairwell, so we are well lit and warm when entering the house. The kids' bedrooms get the east windows—we'd hoped this would gently wake them as the sun rose, but they've learned to draw the drapes and shut out the natural world like the best of us.

Once nighttime falls, most of the modern world wants to stay up to eat, read, binge-watch Netflix, scroll through Instagram, or whatever evening activities we do, so we need to have good, old-fashioned electric light. The most important thing about lighting is that it should be convenient, adequately illuminating, and mostly uninteresting. A few choice fixtures can truly enhance and define a space, but not every room needs an artful grouping of artichoke pendants. Like many things offered to consumers today, there are infinite choices when it comes to lighting. What is important to keep in mind for lighting is its warmth and position. Warmth can actually be measured as well as felt, so you'll likely want to get bulbs in the 2,700 to 3,000 Kelvin range for your home. Kelvin is the measure of color-temperature, and can range from a warm, 1,900K (candles/ambient light) to a cool 6,500K (hospital/industrial light). Daylight is 10,000K,

The pros and cons of the predominant lighting types:

LIGHTING TYPE	BEST LOCATIONS	PROS	CONS
Large pendant	Dramatic and tall spaces like dining rooms and stairwells	Provides focus to a room, lots of light	Can be expensive; need more ceiling height to hang down
Small pendant	Desks, bar counters, dining table	Focused task lighting	Too many can clutter a space; use sparingly for best effect
Recessed can	General lighting in bedrooms, living spaces, hallways, kitchens, bathrooms, exterior roof eaves	Versatile, even lighting, low profile and almost unnoticeable, depending on the chosen trim style	Harder to install, harder to remove
Directional can	Art walls, narrow halls	Focused, directional light where needed	Harder to install and replace
Wall sconces	Halls, exterior doors, bedside in bedrooms, bathroom vanity mirror	Easy to install, ambient lighting, can be a statement piece like small pendants	Need to be careful about placement and height so they don't obstruct space
Surface-mounted ceiling light	Bedrooms, bathrooms	Easy to install and replace; good light coverage and quality	Less design impact; fewer attractive options
Track light	Kitchen, office	Only need one power source for many lights; easy to replace with new fixture in the same track	Track is visible, can look dated
Linear lighting	Office, dining table	Dramatic impact, similar to pendants	Long, skinny form needs to be specific to use
LED rope lights	Outdoor patio, under-cabinet, under railings or cove lighting	Ambient lighting, festive	Low light levels not suited for tasks
String lights	Outdoor	Not just for Christmas anymore!	Are there any?

but it's hard, and perhaps unwise, to mimic natural light artificially.

Then you want to design lighting for the task you are doing. Because we weren't ready to invest in a full lighting package when we were building our house, many of the lights in our house are simple milk glass globes that don't interfere with the visual impact. We're slowly replacing these as we find the right fixtures, but these have served us well and provide a neutral but designed concept. I also like to save the more distinctive light fixtures for spaces that need a focus—stairwells and entry halls are good places because yous're not doing much else in the space. You have a moment to look up and consider the beautiful lighting. Dining tables and bar counters often get special consideration because it's nice to have focused light on your food. Also, the light can hang lower over a table, so you can actually see the light fixture itself in your field of vision.

Recessed lighting fixtures are great for their low-profile, low-cost, high-light impact, but they can also clutter up a ceiling when not carefully laid out. I prefer an evenly spaced row of cans near the walls so the light can bounce off of many surfaces to create even lighting in the room. Dimmers and baffles that direct the lighting toward a wall, desktop, or artwork can also give you more control over the lighting at all times, so make sure these are included in the specs for the house. Some pretend that recessed lighting is invisible and place them scattershot around a room in places that make sense in some ways but might be visually jarring. Placement is definitely something to consider.

As we try to address climate change with sustainability measures,* some states, including California, have very particular requirements regarding energy conservation when it comes to lighting, and countries around the world are phasing out incandescent bulbs altogether. Unfortunately, we did our renovation in that transitional period when incandescent lights were being limited, but LEDs weren't widely available yet, so our "efficient" lighting option was fluorescents. If you don't know these odd shaped bulbs with special base pins that you can never find again, consider them the 8-track cassettes of lighting. They were a bad novelty that was soon superseded by something better. I will only say that when I turn my recessed fluorescents on, it feels like I turned a light off. It makes things look dull. But technology has improved dramatically. New LEDs and broad-spectrum efficient lighting have excellent light quality without sacrificing warmth and comfort.

Lighting can also be one of those deferred design items—you can install simple lights from the hardware store in a jiffy, as we did, then once you've lived in a space for a few months (and recovered from the financial chaos of construction a bit), you can really take the time to choose what you want. The chart on the previous page shows all the pros and cons of the various lighting options available.

*The state of California has goals for the development of zero net-energy buildings, including all new residential construction will be zero net energy (ZNE) by 2020. These are ambitious goals that can only be achieved through the careful design of the energy use of your home.

D-fence.

Remember the old adage that good fences make good neighbors? Well, there was a construction boom going on in my
otherwise quiet neighborhood last year. The din of power
tools and beeps of trucks backing up were a consistent background to the blue jays cackling and children playing. But all
those contractor trucks stacked to the roof rack with building
materials weren't lumbering up our windy potholed streets to
kit out fifty-year-old kitchens with stainless steel ranges and
counter-depth refrigerators as they had for the previous five
years. No, these trucks arrived in droves for the latest craze:
front yard fences. They seemed to be popping up all over the
neighborhood.

Maybe this was a psychological reaction to the housing boom
and insane market escalation of property values, and people
were feeling the need to reclaim even more space. Or perhaps
fences are an attempt at privacy and security in an increasingly public world. With everything from facial recognition to
Google Street View broadcasting your every move to anyone
who cares to look, a fence can offer an added buffer between
you and THEM. Or it's just the realization that there is a lot
of unused space out there! The front yard in the suburban
paradigm has basically been useless. In many neighborhoods
the front lawn set the stage for the look of the house, but large
empty lawns offer little in the way of usability. Why not take
back that space by making it an outdoor extension of your
home? It could become a space for a lush landscaped garden
if you have a green thumb, a play space for lawn bowling, even
a patio for entertaining. This could be done with a fence or

clever garden design to create a sense of privacy while also being as welcoming as you want to be.

Previous generations put a lot of value in the well-kempt grassy front yard—it was symbolic of the American dream, evidence of the pursuit and acquisition of happiness. The suburban house was a miniature version of a castle on its rolling greens. But today, I think we can admit that the deserted front yard has outworn its welcome. Of course, I'm not advocating that front yards become completely private—how antisocial would that be? But we can start to engage the front yard as part of our public and private lives. Use that space, already! The front yard can serve as that intermediate space between inside and outside.

From a design point of view, it's a clever, affordable, and often overlooked way to update the look of your home. You don't always have much of a choice in the style of your home. You may like mission- or craftsman-style homes, but you'll likely get something else when you are limited by the number of bedrooms you need, location, and price. But you can consider a fence your new façade. You may be stuck with a gable roof when you wanted a flat one, or a stucco finish when you wanted wood siding, but a nice cedar fence may do wonders for your psyche as well as your inner modernist.

Our house originally had an old front-yard fence, but those pesky planning codes required that we remove it because it was technically over the property line. We didn't have the space to move it to where it would be legal, so in its place, we allowed a sturdy laurel hedge to grow even taller, providing a green filter to the street beyond. The resulting planted screen offers shade and privacy from the street, but also allows enough interaction with passersby. A wood gate and bell lets people know where to enter. The backyard was a different story. It was open to the neighbors on all sides when we moved in and had a wild, ranch-y look to it. Deer and other wildlife roamed freely, destroying most edibles in their paths. Then, when our neighbor to the back got a survey of her property and realized she had double the land she thought, she decided to enclose her yard so she could have a vegetable garden, chickens, and bees without the wild deer interfering. We were skeptical of losing the openness at first, but now we appreciate it immensely. The fence gently divides the land and provides a backdrop for our own wild playland. I now feel comforted by the marked edge, knowing the kids won't be tumbling down the short cliff beyond.

I'm all for alternatives to fenced-in backyards—like when an entire block opens up their yards to create a super yard for everyone to share. When you see neighborhoods from an airplane, it seems like an obvious and communal solution to problems of space. A small postage-stamp yard may not be enough space for a game of T-ball, but if you combine your yard with your neighbors, it might be! Of course, this type of arrangement only works when yards *and* personalities are compatible. The old adage about fences and neighbors didn't come out of nowhere. However, if you like your neighbor, even smaller moves like a gate between friendly neighbors' yards can expand the idea of privatized space. I don't know how to change the paradigm of each home on its individual lot, with gobs of private outdoor space, but it seems like there are opportunities to expand the concept of how we use it. Some places tend to be settled more densely, and open space is actually a shared amenity—like an Italian piazza or Central Park. Most American cities and towns are more spread out, and we tend to like our own space, and rethinking these boundaries can help to push against that model and give us more of a sense of community.

In-laws, granny flats, studios, and cottages.

In some states like Minneapolis, Oregon, and California, accessory dwelling units (or ADUs in the local planning vernacular) have recently been allowed in more neighborhoods statewide, leading to increased interest for these versatile spaces. ADUs are not a new concept; they've previously been known as in-law units, granny flats, or just that cottage out back. They can be utilized for extra rental income, studio space, a hangout room for your growing teens, a guest room for your visiting relatives, or as a short-term rental (depending on local regulations). ADUs help you expand your space within your existing property. An ADU also offers a model of home and family structure that has been missing in the United States. Previously, we were all expected to start out in a two-parent, single-family home, grow up, move out, and buy our own homes. These days, this model is as inflexible as it is unrealistic to accommodate how we really live. "Kids" are staying home longer, or coming back after some or all of college, and grandparents are helping more and more with grandkids and need their own space to live. A fully functional separate apartment on your property is a great way to keep them close, but not too close. ADUs can also provide much needed housing to a student or other small-home seeker. Check your local regulations and see if they allow them in your neighborhood.

In my practice, we've designed ADUs in many ways, from converting an existing basement into a small studio by adding a bathroom, kitchenette, and patio doors, or as a stand-alone separate little cottage in the backyard. We've also converted a former garage that never held a parked car. These are all good ways to get extra space. Think of it as a tiny home next to your bigger home. More than a couple of clients have used their ADUs as their temporary home while they do a renovation on the main home. Empty-nester clients of mine are building an ADU so they can move into it themselves and rent out the bigger front home to someone who needs the space. The versatility is endless!

How you intend to use the ADU will define how it is designed in relation to your own house. If it will mostly be for you and your extended family, the access between the two homes should be quite seamless—maybe just a separating door and stair. If it's a separate cottage, a shared patio could connect the two homes. If you plan to rent the ADU or want some distance, the interface can be more remote and private. You will want it to feel like a separate home if that is how it will be used.

Designing an ADU is also a nice opportunity to test out design ideas at a smaller scale. It literally is a tiny house, but it has all of the features of a big house: a kitchen(ette), bathroom, bedroom, and living space. I see it as a low-stakes design project, where you can try out a bold color scheme or lighting ideas and see how they work. I envision that we'll be seeing more and more ADUs as cities grapple with rising populations, so we can be innovative with a relatively new housing prototype. We've created eminently livable spaces that are under 400 square feet with big design impacts. We almost always plan for a loft for extra storage or sleeping space and an efficient kitchen layout to maximize the open area. Since space is at such a premium, everything needs to be methodically yet simply designed.

A few things to consider before you think you can just move into your garage tomorrow: the building code actually considers conversion from a garage to a residence as a change of use—meaning it will be held to a higher standard for its structure, air quality, and efficiency. You will most likely need to do quite a bit of upgrading on the garage to make it truly safe and habitable. A new foundation, energy-efficient windows, and proper ventilation are probably all in the cards, so you should plan on the costs of all of this before thinking it will be a quick project. You'll also need to run all of your utilities out there, which is not a cheap proposition. None of this is meant to discourage you—it'll be worth it in the long run to build this out—just be prepared for a "real" project, not a quick weekender.

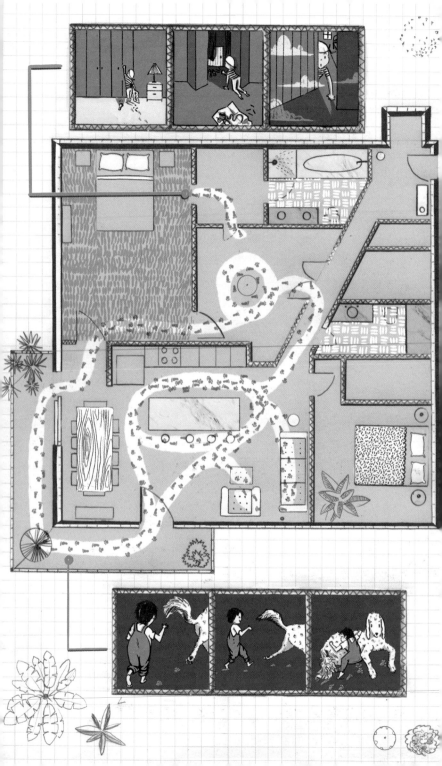

chapter 5

Attention to detail.

Calibrating the little things will make your home yours.

Stuff.

How much stuff do you have? This is a sometimes forgotten yet crucial question that must be asked. In our consumerist culture, it is difficult to avoid the accumulation of things, and there are just so many things to have these days. From kitchen equipment to techno gadgets, there seems to be no end to getting more. Add kids to the mix and you're soon buried in everything from butterfly habitats (we had two) to a full set of "vintage" Star Wars paraphernalia and, of course, a menagerie of stuffed animals. Many of us have even assembled this stuff into certifiable collections.

The architecture of your home should be integrated with the way you live, so this question of stuff and what you do with it is a critical component. Craftsman-style homes are made for accumulation, with built-ins and ledges coming at you from all directions. Those beautiful bookcases are screaming for stuff!* These homes are designed to receive clutter—cabinets and shelves to store things away, deep windowsills for sitting or a small netsuke grouping. Wall paneling and layered-trim details also create more visual nuance in these homes, so by design there literally are more lines in your view. Adding your own stuff is comfortable.

On the other hand, a super-streamlined stark interior with polished concrete floors and smooth white walls will almost slap your hand if you try to leave a napkin on a surface. These clean and austere spaces are less forgiving of leaving some-thing out of place because it is more noticeable. Windows have

*I love Wikipedia's definition of *tchotchke*: "small toys, gewgaws, knickknacks, baubles, lagniappes, trinkets, or kitsch"—it sounds as cluttered as it is.

flush, square edges and no sills so you physically can't clutter them up. Trim is clean, or nonexistent, so your field of vision is uninterrupted. As a design style, I think it looks incredible and feels calming, but it's unsuited to how I actually live. I need a more merciful space to allow some messiness.

I like to think our home veers more toward the approach to stuff of Charles and Ray Eames, the iconic designers of everything from homes to games to movies. Their Los Angeles home was an evolving museum, with rotating displays of their favorite things. Display was selectively designed as part of the architecture. Our home is certainly not as carefully curated, but there is enough to look at. Houseplants occupy windowsills with good southern exposure. Photo collections and artwork have galleries of their own (some may call it a hallway and a stairwell) that are protected from the sun's glare. Souvenirs, art supplies, magazines, and all other mementos of daily life tend to populate selected open shelves. I try to avoid clutter born of every meal and activity of the day, but enough is out to be convenient for how we live, which in turn shows what we love about life. I like to make things that the family uses regularly, be it a favorite puzzle or the hot-water kettle, easily accessible. I'm not kidding anyone by hiding it away in some closet or pantry; I'm only making my life harder by having to put it away every other day. So, instead, these things are put away in plain sight. They have their place so as to reduce clutter, but that place is right there, within grasp. This is not to say everyone would thrive in this way or some other. Many people of a more disciplined nature will gladly put the toaster back in the appliance garage after making their English muffin. No judgment. Just know your proclivities and design accordingly. There are beautiful options for every personality.

Mind you, a hoarders-style problem is not going to be masked by the most creative of architects, but a mild pack rat can be quite comfortable in a well-designed space. The design of the home should accommodate your inclination toward stuff.

The question of stuff also includes how you furnish it. A haphazard collection of furniture accumulated over time is what many of us live with, but once you're designing your new space, consider the pieces that are meaningful in some way and design with those in mind. The rest can be edited out. We've designed around heirloom pieces of family furniture or cherished art so that they get a featured place in the home. That being said, we don't want too rigid a space that can't accommodate future change and dynamism. I think humans like possibilities, so when designing a bedroom or a living room, see if you can make at least two furniture layouts work, using your existing furniture or furniture you plan on getting someday. Our living room is open to the kitchen and dining area, so we've used furniture arrangements that keep the long space either open and unobstructed or more compartmentalized, depending on the placement of couches and tables. Too much furniture is its own version of clutter too, which is why I am a big fan of built-in furniture like bookshelves and benches. Built-ins recede into the architecture and let life take the starring role. A hidden system of shelves and pockets can organize possessions into a cohesive yet subtle visual arrangement.

Kids and other
living creatures.

While kids grow up and eventually outgrow the little things
we do for them, it's nice to incorporate some features into
your home just for them. This doesn't mean that you need to
design a fun house, complete with slides and fireman poles
(I won't stop you), but something as simple as a column in
a space provides endless hours of chasing, climbing, playing
pop goes the weasel, and my son's favorite: "I bet you can't see
me hiding behind this column." Another simple strategy is the
circular plan. A way out of one room and another way back in
is ridiculously fun for the under-eight set. Even I, decidedly
over eight, always like to feel like I have options when I'm in a
space. It can feel claustrophobic to enter a room and have the
only door close behind you. It's not just mob dons who don't
like having their backs to an entry, I think there's something
primal in that logic. I'm sure Neanderthals always kept an eye
on the cave opening to be at the ready for potential intruders.
In my house I probably went overboard with this idea: almost
every room has at least two ways out, including the bathroom.
The kids' rooms even have connecting closets to indulge their
secret passageway fantasies—this we created very simply one
afternoon by knocking down part of the wall that divided
their closets. A couple of hours of using a hammer, a Sawzall,
and a vacuum, *et voilà*! A kid-sized passage (or panic room)
emerged. Now that they are tweens and teens, it's not as well
used a portal, but it was nice while it lasted!

Play that is integrated into the architecture, rather than something we buy (which we do plenty) can be much more satisfying. At our house, a foundation design issue left us with a four-inch gap between our staircase and the wall—my husband's first thought was to design that space as a ramp for our Hot Wheels collection. Yes, it's a little steep for this purpose, and little metal die-cast cars repeatedly crashing down the wall has created a "distressed" look at the bottom of the ramp, but this simple little detail has provided hours of fun for family and visitors over the years.

I generally don't think dedicated playrooms work well—these spaces tend to become overwhelmed with toys. It's a place to hide the stuff rather than enjoy it. Kids would rather play where their parents and siblings and friends are anyway, so living rooms and bedrooms need to be designed for play as well as sleep and rest. This is not to say that your living room should have a train table as its centerpiece, but something as simple as an area rug with a toy bin can provide the nearby respite kids need. All parents know that this discreet toy bin has an insidious way of becoming two or three or ten bins, but eventually toys will not be the focus of your kids' lives, right? Until then and even after, your home can be their true comfort zone.

On a similar note, your pets need some consideration in the design process. Thinking about dog/cat/turtle access before realizing you'll have to cut a nasty hole in your beautiful new people door will make life that much more pleasant. A pet door built into the wall can be convenient and easy to do if it's incorporated during design. It's much easier to install when everything is already open during construction. A place for the pet to eat and another to store pet food should also be considered. Nothing out of an old Fancy Feast commercial is necessary, just a dedicated space that is out of the way yet accessible to your furry friends. If this space becomes an afterthought, you'll be tripping over kibble and slipping on spilled-over water bowls for years to come. Also overlooked is a reasonable place to put the litter box. It's not something anyone wants to think about, but it is also a major issue. A discreet but available area for your feline to do their business will do wonders for your relationships.

These pet needs are part of the inventory of your home that must have a place in your space. If you love fish or reptiles, their aqua/terrariums need a special place in your home for their devoted attendees. If they are too high or too remote or too far from the constant fresh water and supplies they need, you could be looking at a population collapse. Trust me, I speak from experience. When a good friend renovated her house, a new steel beam ran through the new living space— the perfect space to mount a metal birdcage with a very strong magnet! Be creative with your pet needs and you'll all feel comfortable.

Finishing school.

During the housing boom in the early aughts, there was a trend in thinking of homes in terms of resale value instead of as investments in personal futures. Houses were acquired and discarded before you could say option ARM. One byproduct of this mentality was that home improvements were made safe and palatable to a mass market, so you could flip a house on a dime, for many dimes. *Flip This House* and similar shows promoted an aesthetic that could be called the Best of Home Depot. Travertine-esque tile in the bathroom, beige carpets in the bedrooms, and veneer or laminate wood floors everywhere else were standard issue as soon as you entered a Sunday open house. This aesthetic has evolved to be a bit broader and more personal recently as people hunker down in the spaces they have, but all of those remodel shows start to look a little similar, right? A bold graphic bathroom tile, tasteful tile backsplash and white cabinets in the kitchen, wood and metal accents throughout, lots of bright white: this is the current look, and it is certainly lovely. Taste has gotten better, but I want bolder. Don't worry about becoming dated or unfashionable—I would much rather enter a room rich with personal flair and detail than one that looks like all the others.

Something designed as a reflection of a specific time and place can be great if it's done right. The sinewy curves and organic patterns of the Art Nouveau style of the 1920s were done with thought and craftsmanship, and this type of authenticity is still valued today. We don't think of this style as modern now, but at the time it was intended as an expression of the new technologies of indoor lighting and plumbing coming to life. Even a room made entirely of plastic laminate can become a design icon.* The key is a sensitive engagement with your particular tastes and needs and expressing that uniqueness authentically. For instance, a client of mine is an avid surfer and is frequently

*Ralph Wilson was the founder of Wilsonart plastic laminates, and he put his money where his mouth was by creating his entire home out of Formica finishes. The material came to be seen as somewhat cheap or flimsy, but the project is now iconic and timeless. We still use Formica in countless applications.

coming home sandy and salty from a morning surf. Instead of tracking through the house this way, we created a sequence of entry for the him that included board storage, an outdoor shower, and a path back to the house. It resulted in a design feature of the home rather than a quirk.

Finishes, meaning flooring, wall coverings and paint, tiles, and anything else that is the final visible surface applied to the house, are the last but one of the most important features of your home-improvement project. The layout may be beautiful and functional, light may pour in at all the right places, but finishes pull all of these elements together in a cohesive whole. I often think about the *Big Lebowski* line, and how the infamous stolen rug "really tied the room together." It's true. Rugs can tie the room together and define a space. (A rug is technically not a "finish" since it is not attached to the house, but you get my point, right?) This is also the time when you can diverge from your architect or designer. This is one area I may not be quite aligned with my fellow architects. I am happy to choose finishes for clients, but I want the space to look like their space, not mine. When I do work with my clients on the interior finishes, I take into account the personal tastes and proclivities of the homeowner. I was thrilled when a recent client that had a bubbly personality liked the sunny yellow cabinets we presented for her kitchen. It was a perfect match, and unlike any other home. We are all so different, and hopefully our homes can reflect this.

How you go about choosing finishes can be daunting for anyone, and I've seen the gamut in how this gets accomplished in a project. Sometimes homeowners start finding what they like early on in a project, and the design team can work to incorporate that vision. Others aren't comfortable with designing interiors and want more assistance from their architect or interior designer. Some have no interest in designing anything at all, and completely trust the designer to do all of the interiors, down to the furniture, throw pillows, and art on the walls. All of these are fine, and you should do what works for you, but I encourage you to trust yourself, and make your space your own. Be bold.

Crafting your home interiors is an opportunity to really consider what your home means to you and the type of space you want to live in. It's a place that provides you with your most basic needs, from shelter to nourishment to comfort. The most immediate and cost-effective impact on a space is color. Paint is a very forgiving design element that can change and evolve with you. Entire books are written on color theory, and all the big paint companies declare their "color of the year," well, yearly, so I won't go into what color means. A question to consider instead is, what does color mean to you? Suffice it to say that we have so much choice in color now, and you can use it to help set the mood of a space. You'll notice many home décor Instagram accounts and online resources feature bright-white interiors with selective color "pops." These images are very seductive, but do white walls deliver the carefree and casual life the pictures claim? Certainly for some. But white can be harder to maintain and less forgiving in everyday life. We chose a white for most of our home, but it shows more of our life than I'd care to admit: scuff marks along the chair line,* splattered of paint from an art project gone awry. Yes, we clearly need to be on top of it more, but a nice light gray

*Chair scuffs are why wood wainscoting and chair rails are a great option where they make sense.

may give us a little more cover for the everyday toll the walls take. We're repainting soon and will deepen our color choices where the walls get the most contact. When a room is a deep hue, like the colors of antique books, it can feel fuller and warmer. Light colors reach out and brighten a room. The wall color can also start to pick up the colors of other things in the room and bring it all together, in much the same way a rug can. Also, let's reconsider the adherence to flat sheen finishes for all paint. Add a little shine to your day, at least in some instances. A satin finish is just a bit easier to clean than full-on flat. Museums are able to use flat white because they repaint constantly. My house is no museum.

More permanent finishes like bathroom tile and wood floors can't be easily changed like paint, but I still recommend that you seek authenticity and personality in these choices. You can start from a practical viewpoint like durability or cleanability, each of which will steer you in different directions. Or you can start from nostalgia and emotion—does a certain finish remind you of a fond place in your memory? My family used to go to my mother's childhood home in a remote, hilly part of eastern India when I was a kid, and I still remember the wood floors there. They were knotted and creaky, and I'm sure I could feel chilly air coming up between the boards. And they felt like home. It's okay to use whatever criteria is important to you in choosing finishes, to create the space and feel you want. The other finish I remember fondly is a geometric tile at my aunt's house. It was a tile that could be positioned in different ways to create different patterns, Escher-like. I searched for ages to replicate this tile, and now it's suddenly everywhere! Any HGTV or Pinterest superfan will tell you we are in the middle of a tile renaissance right now. For years, all we could get was the basic ceramic glazed tile in a few different sizes and colors. We could add some glass mosaic accent stripes and borders and call it a day. Back in the day, we actually had to go to Mexico to get Mexican tiles, Marrakesh for Moroccan ones. Today, tile, like many products, has returned as a true artistic craft, with both local artisans and big companies offering gorgeous lines in all price ranges. We were able to find a beautiful patterned cement floor tile, and our bathroom now reminds me of my childhood.

As I've advocated in other parts of this book, the point is to create a space that works for you. Options are literally endless, and this doesn't necessarily make things easier. Fewer choices may be limiting, but it also can force creativity. If you ever saw that short-lived magazine *Nest: A Quarterly of Interiors*, from the turn of this century, it featured unusual interiors born of individuality and creativity, and often born of necessity. There was a modest dwelling in Africa where the owner had used bottle caps hammered into tarp surfaces to create texture and color. The magazine featured eclectic collections and eccentric personalities. The magazine brought professional photography and page layout to previously uncelebrated interiors—and isn't this where we all live? In uncelebrated interiors? I'm in favor of showing off your personality in your home. This certainly already comes through once you live in a space, but design and architecture are integral to how you express yourself.

The little things.

When you've completed construction and you've settled
into your new abode, things that may not have been on your
radar too much during the design and construction process
will suddenly be magnified as big as day once you're using
them all the time. Little revelations will surface—some good,
some frustrating, and some downright flabbergasting. It's the
light switches, the heat registers, the cabinet-door hinges,
the height of shelves, door swings—things that may have
been "designed" during construction or not really designed
at all. Often, things have changed from the design on paper
during construction because of unforeseen conditions, or
field changes, or it just didn't work out as planned for various
reasons. This could have happened with the blessing of your
architect, but you didn't hear about it, or your contractor had
to make an executive decision for some reason or other. Some
examples:

- My three kids all huddle around a single heat register
  that happens to be under the breakfast table. Being the
  one closest to the furnace, it's the hottest and the most
  accessible, so they push and pull and cry to get their
  little toes a square inch of that glorious heat on brisk
  mornings. Two other registers not fifteen feet away
  simply won't do!

- My sister-in-law had a custom cabinet designed for her
  kids' room to minimize the clutter of toys. Unfortunately,
  their builder made the cubbies *exactly* the same size as the
  baskets that were to be inserted, leaving no room for even
  the tiniest hands to pull them out.

- Our light switches are scattered around our open floor plan like a sniper shot them there at random, leaving us turning them on and off until we find the right one. My husband wishes we had one giant lever that would just shut everything down. Instead, every night we perform an intricate choreography of turning off lights around the house. Bob Fosse would take notes.

- All cooking smells from our beautiful open kitchen waft right up our stairwell to the front door, so anyone walking in will immediately know what we are having for dinner. Simmering chicken soup can be comforting and warm for our visitors, but we don't always want to advertise the buttered popcorn and burnt toast! The range hood and slew of range-adjacent windows just do not do their jobs.

EGADS! How to solve these seemingly simple problems?! One option is to accept and become Zen-like—let these inconveniences wash over you in the light of the rest of your fabulous home. We have come to terms with the heat registers this way. In retrospect, we should have installed radiant heating, which delivers even heat instead of hot spots. But alas, we survive. However, there is another option to address these issues: Communication, Checking in with the team, and Constant diligence during construction. At our house, the scattered switches are completely my fault. I walked the house with the electrician, confirming locations that seemed to make sense as he convincingly talked me through it. I also became hyperaware that each switch/outlet/data point had a dollar amount attached to it, so I thought I was being efficient. We ignored the electrical plan I had so meticulously created, and I let the builder take charge, thinking he had built more houses than I had and probably knew better. I should have considered that he had never built *my* house before, and we had a more accurate idea of how we wanted to live in the space.

My in-laws' cabinet flaws are likely a series of miscommunications—different people in the process probably got different information. My sister-in-law asks for cubbies to fit her baskets—the contractor takes note and tells the cabinetmaker the cubby size without mentioning their purpose—the cabinetmaker makes the cubbies based on the information he has. It's all a game of telephone if everyone is not looped in. Ideally, the architect would have drawn up the proposed shelving system, with dimensions and materials noted. Architects are supposed to take into account all of the different pieces of information that go into a built piece, and coordinate them into a lovely, cohesive creation. Then the cabinetmaker reviews this design, and does his own drawing, called a "shop drawing" that describes exactly how he is going to build it, for the owner and architect's approval. You'd think drawing things twice would be redundant, but it's the best process for ensuring things get built as designed. The shop drawing may propose changes because something designed is unfeasible or a material is over the budget or out of stock. We've received shop drawings that look nothing like the design intent shown in the architectural drawings, and we mark these up with revisions and send them back. Sometimes changes proposed by the contractor are good and appropriate, which is why it's important to have this step. This process is helpful for simple pieces where we're only working with one trade, and absolutely essential for complex designed systems that coordinate multiple trades—like a custom steel staircase with metal, wood, electrical, and framing contractors all involved in making the design come together. The cabinet issue my in-laws had could have been caught sooner if they'd had a chance to review what they were getting before it was all said and done.

Ask a question when something doesn't make sense. As the homeowner, you are more invested than anyone in the outcome, so you need to be heard at every step. You're definitely not the only one who is doing this for the first time, because every project is unique. The lesson to be learned is that the devil or god (or whoever you fear more) is in the details. On large projects financed with developers or public agencies, this process of involvement is clearly defined through weekly owner-architect-contractor meetings in which all questions are formally submitted to the design team, and I suggest you do a version of this for a residential project as well. It's good to get everyone together at regular intervals to check on status and answer any questions. Without this check-in, the contractor may move ahead with something he isn't sure about just to keep on schedule. The meeting helps bring accountability to everyone. It doesn't need to be formal. You can just talk and walk through the site, and the contractor can let you know what's coming up, and what decisions might need to be made. He may have questions on drawings that aren't clear or on the scope of something that's been left out.

The best way to deal with the inherent translation issues when you move from drawings to buildings is communication.

Sometimes architects aren't contracted to stay involved during construction, which saves some money for the owner, but unless the owner knows the drawings really well and knows how things get built, there will be some dropped balls. There are various levels of service from an architect, from reviewing every single item that comes on-site, to occasional meetings and assistance as needed. Renovation projects as a rule will run into unexpected issues, like wood rot in a wall, or a pipe that shouldn't be there, and your architect and contractor as a team can help figure out the best path forward. There are also design modifications made during construction that can actually improve a project, but these will be missed opportunities if all eyes aren't on the problem.

Your architect is your advocate during construction, and the drawings prepared by him or her *are* the contract. Some builders will follow the direction of the drawings to a T, while others regard them as mere guidelines. How do you navigate the range of services available for your particular project? Again, communication is key. All of the team players—owner, architect, and contractor—need to be in the same room and set the tone for the project. Weekly meetings keep everyone on the same page. With a typical contract for construction provided by the American Institute of Architects, the contractor is supposed to issue "submittals" for every item specified in the drawings to the architect for final approval. For instance, the final sample of cedar siding is given to the architect to review. The architect confirms this complies with what is in the drawings and approves the sample. Clearly, this process adds time and costs to a project. Most residential projects I've worked on do not have this level of service, but as I said, coordination and communication during construction help the outcomes of the project align with the vision that was so carefully crafted during design. Why go through all of the work of design, only to see it fall apart?

The following chart shows the trifecta of effective and essential communication during construction to keep a project on track.

Essential elements for construction communication:

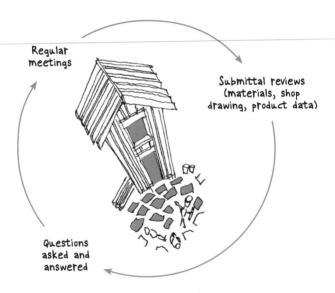

Regular meetings

Submittal reviews (materials, shop drawing, product data)

Questions asked and answered

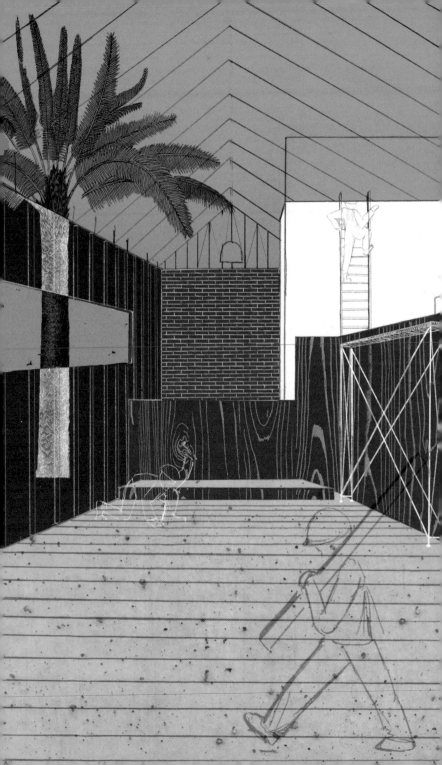

chapter 6

Controlled chaos, otherwise known as construction.

When it all starts to come together. First it falls apart a little, but it *will* come together.

Paper architecture.

When you were interviewing architects and getting proposals from them, you may have thought you were getting the same thing from any one of them, but it can be hard to parse out and compare what's what. We all use different standard contracts and different descriptions of work. You'll probably see these terms on the contract:

- schematic design
- design development
- construction documents

Each of these is a progressively more complex and complete phase of drawings that you can use for permitting, bidding, and eventually construction. But what will go into each of those phases? Hopefully these will be described in detail in the contract, but you can also ask if the drawings will include:

- cabinet details
- trim details
- finish, window, and door schedules
- lighting and electrical plans
- design details

That's a short list of items that can get excluded from construction drawings because they aren't always required for building permits, so see if they're included when talking to architects. You'll want as much information as possible to get accurate bids and a clear picture of what you want. You'll also want to know how the architects typically handle construction. There are varying levels of involvement, and I suggest you at least have the architect on-site every couple of weeks to take a look at the progress and answer any questions that have come up. Architects will know the drawings better than anyone, so deviations will be more apparent to them, and they can have work corrected before it's too late.

On the other hand, if you're planning for more of a DIY project, where you will be getting prefab cabinets and choosing your own finishes, maybe even building walls yourself, you can ask for a more basic set of drawings—some call it a "builder's set"—meaning it's enough to build from but it doesn't go into a lot of additional details. This is fine if you're going to be very involved in construction and will be there to answer the inevitable questions that will arise from limited drawings. You can save a little upfront money and get moving on construction.

When you get bids from contractors you'll also want to look for where there are holes in their bids. Are they tying their contract to the drawings? This is preferred so that they are required to build what's described there. Otherwise you may get pushback when you're wondering why the custom bookcase you have in the drawings arrives on-site as prefab shelves on metal wall standards. They may also provide "allowances" for work that isn't decided yet, like door hardware or finishes. This means that they are plugging in an assumed number while you decide what you want. This can be a source of cost increases because they may have called for a cheap tile in their estimate when you actually wanted stone. Allowances are typical, just be aware that this number will change based on your final choices. The third thing to look for is exclusions. These are items that are specifically not included in the bid and may include things like prefabricated cabinets or extensive drainage or site work. These are big-ticket items, so you want to make sure you're setting aside enough that you'll be able to purchase these on your own if needed. Some contractors will take on these items in their bid, but construction contracts run the gamut for residential work, so be aware.

Paper architecture to me is like a paper doll. You're getting a mini, flat version of your future home. You want it to give you a fairly accurate picture of your future home, so the drawings should be thorough and detailed enough so you know what to expect after construction.

Get detailed bids from contractors or be your own.

Once you've completed the design phase, and you're in possession of a bunch of drawings, you're ready to build! It's amazing to realize all the expense and time that went into the design of your home before anyone's even touched a hammer, but this is what it takes to get the project to be built properly. There was an era when a builder would arrive on a site and start building a wall where it seemed to make sense with direction from the ruler, or his architect.* Since at least the

*Imhotep was the ancient Egyptian architect of the earliest pyramids and is sometimes credited with being the first architect.

Renaissance, when architecture, like so many other things, flourished, there have been drawings to build from. A builder needs the plans of a project drawn with as much detail as possible to (1) provide an accurate bid, and (2) build it correctly. Most contractors won't be able to get you an accurate price for the job until they see the detailed architectural and structural drawings. I realize it feels like putting the cart before the horse to completely design your home before you know how much it will cost, but you can usually get some ballpark pricing from your architect or builder based on a square-footage cost or a preliminary set of plans. Square-footage costs, unfortunately, don't take into account the nuances of a project, like if you have a lot of special cabinet details or a large new kitchen. These all add to the project cost, and it may not get picked up accurately until it's truly bid out. I've seen costs jump from a ballpark figure of $300 per square foot up to $400 per square foot once the design is fleshed out in drawings and the true scope is evident—so it can be a big shock! You can also bring in contractors early on to provide real-time pricing of the design using their market knowledge, though they'll likely charge you for this service. It may well be worth it in some cases.

Toward the beginning of the design process for your home-improvement project, figure out with your architect what type of construction contract you will be working with. The typical format is design-bid-build, which means that you and your architect will design the project exactly the way you want it, with all the details worked out, then you will bid out the project to a few contractors, and you'll choose the best offer, based on price, experience, and reputation.

Another option is a design/build team, where architecture and construction are one entity that works together. This can eliminate some conflicts between architects and contractors, but this process has its own drawbacks. Design/build teams often have a tried-and-true way of building, so you may not get the innovation or options you get from independent teams. Also, your architect is typically the owner's advocate during construction, so when your architect and contractor are a single entity you are not really getting an unbiased opinion. However, if you like what you see with their previous work, this is an efficient means to an end.

In between these options is selecting your contractor before the design is complete. This way, the contractor has input on cost, schedules, and material availability in real time. There may be a construction cost increase here because there is little incentive to low-bid a job you already have, but building trust throughout the design process is incredibly valuable. In my opinion, this is the best option because you will get a builder who really knows the project and why certain decisions were made.

If you are very organized and have a lot of extra time, consider being your own general contractor (GC). As a homeowner, you are legally entitled to contract your own home construction (check your local regulations), and you don't necessarily need to know everything about construction. We started our project thinking we would find a good general contractor to build it out, but once we started getting bids, it was clear that we could not afford any one of them. So we made some simplifications to the design and started getting bids for foundations. We didn't have bids beyond that, but we needed the concrete pouring done lickety-split before the rainy season. So we picked the best and most available foundation team we could find (on the recommendation of our structural engineer, so it wasn't a total gamble) and hoped for the best. We started getting other bids as the foundation was underway, the most pressing being the wall and roof framing, which was coming up next. This ended up being the hardest trade to get bids for, since most general contractors seem to do this work themselves. We ended up having the foundation team do the framing too. They were not as good at framing as they were at foundations, but since our construction was pretty typical wood framing, it worked out fine. We made decisions as we went and coordinated up to four teams of workers on any given day. It was a lot of management, but we saved about 20 percent in cost and overhead that a general contractor would have charged, and we picked most subcontractors on recommendations, flexibility, and cost rather than prior relationships. Most general contractors have working relationships with all of their subcontractors and can rely on them to show up for each job, so though we were at a bit of a disadvantage cold-calling subs who had never heard of us, most were eager to work.

Being your own GC is definitely not for everyone, though. I had to be on-site every day (not too much of a problem for me since we were living upstairs and I worked from home), answering questions and directing the work, often with a baby on my hip. This constant interaction is critical to a successful project. Since we were on a budget, we mostly hired affordable subcontractors who didn't always have the most skilled employees for our job. In fact, many of these employees were shockingly *unskilled* in what needed to be done. They were left at the site by their supervisors with a drill and confused look on their faces, leaving me to tell them their job for the day. Occasional language barriers also required me to pantomime instructions, which was probably a funny thing to see, but was a frustrating experience nonetheless. Subcontractors are a mixed bag, to say the least. This inconsistency is why general contractors have their go-to guys for subcontracts—they've been through this and have vetted the best options for them.

It will work out in the end, but don't expect everything to be done right unless you tell them what your version of "right" is. Do you want your bathroom light to be centered above the sink? You would think that could be left unsaid, but it can't. Are you going to have wall-mounted cabinets in your kitchen? You can't add support for those after the drywall is in. All of these things may be referenced in your architectural drawings, but, again, many subcontractors don't even look at those. It is your job as a general contractor to know what the drawings call for, then to make sure it is done accordingly. You may be rushing out to buy fixtures that need to be installed that day, or making snap decisions about design changes, so be prepared for some chaos. Make friends with spreadsheets.

Being my own GC on my home improvement was an eye-opening experience, and I gained a much better understanding of the depth and complexity of construction. I see why it's so important to have someone who is organized and has experience. If a GC has long-established relationships with their subs, those subs are more likely to prioritize your project and do a good job. It's all about relationships. For me, an unknown entity trying to build her own home, I had to be scrappy and resourceful. I may not do it again for a big project, but I'm glad I did it once to see how important this job is. I have a current client who is contracting her own home, and she likes it so much she's thinking of getting licensed to do it for others. Hurray!

Being your own contractor:

If you decide to be your own contractor, these are the trades you will need to coordinate, at minimum; this is a partial list of typical subcontractors needed for a project. There may be others for specialty items and IT or AV needs:

- ☐ shoring
- ☐ excavation
- ☐ concrete
- ☐ waterproofing
- ☐ plumbing
- ☐ electrical
- ☐ mechanical
- ☐ roofing
- ☐ drywall
- ☐ finish carpentry
- ☐ tile
- ☐ flooring
- ☐ cabinetmakers/installers
- ☐ windows and doors
- ☐ exterior finishes
- ☐ painting
- ☐ landscaping and exterior work

If this list isn't daunting, contracting your home may be right for you!

Decisions, decisions.

Heading into construction, get ready for decision overload.
During the design process, you probably didn't already pick
out all of your plumbing fixtures, door handles, tile, and
appliances with your architect, but these are decisions that
will need to be made at a fast clip if you want construction to
keep pace. It's never too early to start pondering these things.
A lot of my clients don't want to think about the towel rack
they want before starting construction, and in some ways
that's not a bad way to go. You can stay nimble and get things
that are available or new or on sale, rather than committing to
something that may not be available later on or that you may
not like by the time construction rolls around. Construction
is so far out from the design phase that the cool wallpaper you
were salivating over during design suddenly seems lackluster,
or worse, *everywhere*. You will hopefully at least have chosen
the type of products, if not the specific product. For instance,
you'll want to know from the beginning if you have any gas
appliances so you can plan for it.*

All the decisions that you need to make can get overwhelming. It even has a boring name: decision fatigue. Spreadsheets
can help keep you organized, but I think the most important
thing is to have a diagram or guiding principle for your home.
Some may call this guiding principle a design concept or style,
or maybe you call it an origin story—how did your home
come to be yours—but essentially, it's a way to decide on the

*Some cities are moving toward banning or at least limiting gas appliances in new
construction, so you'll want to check on this with your local jurisdiction before
deciding.

look of your home. This way, decisions can follow a path, and you won't be swayed by every pretty thing that comes into view. There are many things you are going to like as you start deciding what will be permanently installed in your home, so use the idea of the guiding principle as a chance to narrow down the options. This is when style can come in handy—if you're sticking with a Danish modern design theme for the home, then all of the fixtures and finishes need to align with that theme to create a cohesive home. You can filter your searches to exclude ornate light fixtures and prioritize natural woods and white tones. You can also develop a set of criteria with your architect, such as "I'm doing supergraphic themes in this project," and you keep in mind features that resonate or support this concept, from paint color to faucets to lights. If you have a bold graphic on the walls, you probably don't want a competing pendant light hanging in front of it. Or maybe your guiding principle is a single word like "comfort." If you develop this process for your home, then the decision-making can fall in place.

If you didn't make all of the necessary choices during design (see "Paper architecture" and what gets included in the different phases), which is not uncommon in residential projects, a handy partial list of what you'll need to look into and decide on is on the next page. You can hand this decision-making over to your architect or interior designer, and he or she can develop the design. Your contractor may even come to you with what he recommends and prefers installing, but ultimately you'll need to sign off on these items in addition to any furniture and built-ins that were already designed or planned.

Choices by space:

Bathroom(s)
Toilet, sink and/or vanity (custom or prefab), faucets (sink and tub), tub, showerhead, mixing valves, tile (floor and wall), baseboards, thresholds, shower drain, mirror, medicine cabinet, lighting, switch and outlet type, accessories like towel racks, robe hooks, TP holder. Phew.

Kitchen
Cabinet type (custom or semi-custom or prefab), final cabinet layout including specialty items like lazy Susans, spice racks, trash bins, countertop material and edge details, sinks, faucets, cabinet hardware, appliances (fridge, dishwasher, garbage disposal, oven, range, microwave, anything else special you want), backsplash, lighting (task, overhead, and specialty), flooring. Deep breath.

Bedrooms (it gets a little easier here)
Lighting (overhead and bedside), wall coverings, flooring, media support (outlets, data ports, cable, etc.)

Living room
General lighting, task and specialty lighting, wall covering, flooring, media support, fireplace and/or mantle, built-ins

Dining room
Table lighting, general lighting, wall covering, flooring

As you can see, kitchens and bathrooms are the most design-intensive spaces, but all rooms have decisions that need to be made, and this is only a partial list. Architects and designers have various ways of organizing this information into schedules and drawings. Most important, though, is to have fun and make these decisions with intention and authenticity.

The art of trim.

When it comes to interiors, seamless, trimless clean details make so much visual sense to me, but the reality of today's construction industry is that trim covers up where the seams appear in standard construction methods. Drywall doesn't generally end cleanly at the floor, flooring doesn't butt up against the wall, doors and windows are shimmed into place, electrical outlets are roughed in at framing, with covers added after drywall. Trim—like baseboards, moldings, switch plates, and lots and lots of caulk—covers all of the slop at these otherwise ghastly joints. All contractors will charge more for eliminating these seams without using trim, so decide if this is really where you want to spend your money. It takes a real craftsman with experience and an eye for modern detail to create beautiful deceptively simple features. For example, flush baseboard details are de rigueur among modern designs. This is where the wall finish (drywall or otherwise) is set flush with the baseboard, which is typically a flat piece of wood or metal. The effect is subtle but elegant and creates a single discernible line along walls rather than the visual clutter created by traditional fussy base and crown moldings. Between these two finishes is a metal reglet, a discreet trim piece that often is not noticed by the casual viewer. It receives the drywall above and the trim below. Each material must be cut perfectly to fit in the reglet channel. In this detail, the baseboard is not really trim at all, but a true toe-kick protection for the wall. Similar clean lines can be achieved at all intersections of materials, all requiring a similar level of skill. So, you can see that these details are going to cost much more than standard methods. Simplicity is deceptive—and is sometimes worth it. Your typical laborers are not skilled enough to do this level of work, but they probably can rip down lengths of prefinished wood and attach them to your wall to create a clean window detail.

We had to forgo this level of detail for the most part at our house because the contractor for finishes was somewhat inexperienced in construction—it was me and my husband. So we chose clean lines when we could, and also allowed ourselves some tolerance while we learned on the job. Our drywall contractor was able to execute a very simple trim-less detail at exterior doors and windows, but otherwise we let baseboards cover up where the bamboo floor meets the drywall, grout and caulk fills in some gaps in our stair-riser tile, and door casing covers the shims positioning our doors.

The trim and transitions from one material to another, is one of the defining features of many styles of homes. A simple flat trim with square edges is great for a modern airy look, while more elaborate rosettes and fluted, tiered moldings work with historic homes. Mission style and some modern styles often use a hidden door frame detail that makes the door look like there isn't any trim at all (called a kerfed door jamb). Rounded or square edges can set off different styles too. Trim really can set the tone for the home, so make sure these details are included in the design. In craftsman homes, the trim almost *is* the design. We spent a lot of time trying to match existing trim in a recent craftsman home project. We couldn't use the same beautiful gumwood used on the original home, but we found a very close approximation through trial and error of sampling different woods and stains. We also used a simplified shape in the new areas of work—the intricacy of the original was hard to replicate, and we didn't want to fake it. A simpler copy was the preferred route in this case.

On a similar note, exposed industrial equipment like steel heating ducts aren't your run-of-the-mill insulated ducts just left exposed (if only it were that easy), but they are a different beast altogether. Plan ahead with your architect to make sure this works out the way you envision. "Regular" residential ducts are something akin to stuffed black trash bags that then get shoved into your ceiling space to deliver that precious warmth. The exposed, laissez-faire look of an urban loft with ducts and pipes and beams running every which way has been designed that way. In other words, not designing something doesn't necessarily make it look that way. The look of expedience and ease is usually the result of a vigilantly crafted design.

The exterior of a home is similarly defined by how its edges come together. If you have wood siding, are the corners mitered (cut at a 45-degree angle so the corner can meet at a single line) or overlapped and covered with a trim board? Or do they butt up against a block corner piece? There are many ways to finish a corner, and each one results in a different look! How that siding meets a window is another conversation altogether. Is it a wide flat trim, or a minimal sliver? These are just ideas for siding in general, not even considering all of the shapes, sizes, wood species, and textures available. Cement plasters, stones, and metals are similarly varied in their installations. Most homeowners will leave these minutiae up to their architect, but it's good to start noticing how the homes you see are put together.

Before we moved into our house, it was a white stucco box with teal-wood siding accents in a couple of areas. Yes, it was a little *Miami Vice*, but we didn't veer too far from this in the renovation. Since we added new plywood shear walls* throughout the existing walls, we had to replace the exterior finishes. We liked the stucco-and-wood combination and basically kept this style while modernizing the colors. We have no-maintenance gray cement plaster, which also creates a fire-safe finish† on most of the house, and warmer painted wood at the entryway where people are actually up close to the siding. The way these materials come together echoes the casual, modern style of the interior. Our details are not too difficult to create, and the effect is comfortable and unfussy.

*The joys of living in earthquake country!

†Cool roofs are literally light-colored or reflective roofing materials designed to reflect heat and sunlight away from your house. If all homes had cool roofs, there would be a collective positive effect on the environment and temperature.

In conclusion . . .

Improving your home is a daunting but gratifying mission.
When my husband and I bought our home, we thought of it
as our own little Case Study House*—where our ideas would
be tested and construction endured for the good of human-
ity—well, something like that. We were limited most by time
and money, as most American families are, but we were also
committed to creating a home for our family that would serve
us for our own eternity. The decisions we made were never life
or death but were instead based on simple ideas about how we
wanted to and could live in our home. We had to stay nimble
in our decision-making among changing circumstances.
Ultimately, our home is a reflection of our evolving selves.

Through this building process, the things about modern
architecture and design that I've come to value most are not so
much about the look, but the life. Modernism's original reputation was based on white walls and minimalism—with life as
a performance piece against this backdrop. Modernism today
is also about smart construction, honesty about your needs,
and allowing yourself the space to just be.

Beyond building your dream house, our modernity is also
about change and evolution. What you need as a struggling
single barista or intern will morph if you get a partner, pets,
kids, or a new job. For many of us, these changes force us to
become nomadic—moving to a new city or house or apartment every time our needs change. In buying a house, we

*Sponsored by *Arts & Architecture* magazine in the late 1940s, the Case Study Houses,
mostly built in Los Angeles, were experiments in American residential architecture.
Major architects of the time were commissioned to design and build affordable, well-
designed model homes. These experiments resulted in some of the most iconic homes
of the midcentury era and came to define the style.

committed ourselves to staying in one place for a long time, but yet, our needs still evolve. Nothing in a home should be so precious that it interferes with daily life.

We crafted our home with the understanding that our needs can and will change, and the home will adapt. We see it as a constantly developing organism that grows with us. Even in the short fifteen years we've called it home, the space has needed to change for us. The kids have grown and we added doors to the open-plan home office, turning it into an extra bedroom. It works great for now. I'm also thinking about the future: How can my husband and I accommodate our parents moving in with us if needed—how do we create or change that space? It's a constant tinkering to become aligned with how we live now and how we might live in the future.

The *dynamic home* may best describe our approach. It's growing with us.

Acknowledgments

It takes so many people to encourage and push a creative project along, especially when it's not your day job. First, I want to thank my husband, Mike, who is thankfully not an architect. He always provided an outsider's point of view. His lighthanded review of all iterations of the book let the content emerge. My children gave me the space to work when I needed to. My oldest daughter, Hera Wetzel, a Gen-Zer, helped with the style quiz, inserting her pop-culture and music knowledge, and wry humor. She also created the illustrations of the house styles in the quiz. My childhood friend Melinda Joe, who is a food, wine, and sake journalist, gave me invaluable feedback at the on the style and accessibility of the book. My mother-in-law, Jane Wetzel, was perhaps my greatest cheerleader. I had a version of this book that was just for clients and friends, and she ordered dozens of these and passed them around her friend groups and even left copies on a cruise ship in Europe. Who knows where they ended up! My kids' elementary schoolteacher Adria Rosen read a draft and told her students all about it, impressing my son and spurring me to consider publishing. I'm lucky enough to have writer friends who offered constructive advice along the way—Adam Mansbach, Laura Lambert, Karin Spirn, and Gary Wolf. Rachel Neumann was the first to see publishing potential in this, and I'll be forever grateful to her for bringing it to my wonderful team at Shambhala, including my editor, Audra Figgins, who thoughtfully shepherded the book to its final, refined state. And finally, my parents, Rani and Kalyan Dutta-Choudhury and sister, Amrita, who shaped who I am today. They are models of doing things your own way and being authentic in speech and action.

About the author

Devi has been studying, designing, and thinking about architecture for most of her life. Having lived in varied environments—from college towns to Himalayan villages, Southern suburbia to coastal cities—Devi credits these cross-cultural experiences with shaping her understanding of lifestyles and the homes that support them. She attended Tulane University and UCLA, where she received her two master's degrees in architecture. She now lives in Berkeley, California, where she started her own full-service architecture practice in 2009, specializing in modern, casual design. She enjoys working on a range of housing types from larger multi-family, co-living, and workforce housing to townhouses and single-family homes. She's active in local planning and advocacy efforts that support a diverse and dynamic built environment. She loves working on homes the most because of the personal relationships she develops with the clients, helping them live more meaningful and realized lives in their new space.